June T Trafton
Apt A
156 W 74th St
New York, NY 10023

D1523237

A SPIRIT OF INQUIRY
COMMUNICATION IN PSYCHOANALYSIS

Psychoanalytic Inquiry Book Series

Volume 19

Psychoanalytic Inquiry
Book Series

A SPIRIT OF INQUIRY
COMMUNICATION IN PSYCHOANALYSIS

JOSEPH D. LICHTENBERG
FRANK M. LACHMANN
JAMES L. FOSSHAGE

THE ANALYTIC PRESS
2002   Hillsdale, NJ   London

The clinical vignette described on pages 95 to 97 in chapter 4 was published previously as: J. Fosshage (1997), "Listening/experiencing perspectives and the quest for a facilitative responsiveness" in *Conversations in Self Psychology: Progress in Self Psychology, Vol. 13*, ed. A. Goldberg (Hillsdale, NJ: The Analytic Press, pp. 33–55). Portions of chapter 5 appeared in *Selbstpsychologie*, 5/6:276–304, 2001; portions of chapter 6 appeared in *Selbstpsychologie*, 3/2:44–74, 2001; and portions of chapter 7 appeared in *Psychoanalytic Inquiry*, 3:279–294, 1983.

Published by The Analytic Press, Inc.
101 West Street, Hillsdale, NJ 07642
www.analyticpress.com

Designed and typeset by Compudesign, Charlottesville, VA

Index by Leonard Rosenbaum, Washington, DC

Library of Congress Cataloging-in-Publication Data

Lichtenberg, Joseph D.
   A spirit of inquiry: communication in psychoanalysis / Joseph D. Lichtenberg, Frank M. Lachmann, James L. Fosshage
      p. ; cm. — (Psychoanalytic inquiry book series; v. 19)
   Includes bibliographical references and index.
   ISBN 0-88163-364-X
      1. Psychoanalysis.   2. Psychotherapist and patient.
   3. Interpersonal communication.   I. Lachmann, Frank M.
   II. Fosshage, James L.   III. Title,   IV. Series.
   [DNLM: 1. Communication. 2. Psychoanalysis. 3. Physician-Patient Relations. WM 460.5.C5 L699s 2002]
   RC506.L5238 2002
   616.89'17-dc21

                                                        2002074796

Printed in the United States of America

10   9   8   7   6   5   4   3   2   1

CONTENTS

INTRODUCTION

From its inception, psychoanalysis has been and is a depth psychology, a voyage of discovery conducted in a spirit of inquiry. The couch, the frequency of meetings, and the talking became its vehicles. Historically, the patient free associated and a talking cure resulted from the cathartic effect. Thus, communication, that is, talking and being listened to, was a given. However, the talk between analyst and analysand was found to be a complex form of communication that called for further inquiry. An appreciation of this complexity led to the study of defense and resistance, the deceptions of everyday life. These deceptions interfered with free and full revelation of prior and current experiences. Their occurrence was explained according to a theory of drive distortion, primary or secondary repression, and a catalogue of "mechanisms" of defense. Communications were divided into "manifest" and "latent." What appeared to be manifest was not regarded as relevant. What was latent and could not be said was assumed to be expressed through transference phenomena or gesture, a topic to which we return in chapter 3. When wishes, desires, and intentions were spoken, they were open to interpretation, and through interpretation and reconstruction, salient past events, traumas, and distortions were uncovered and discovered. When enacted instead of spoken, however, the unconscious wishes, desires and intentions might be recognized by the analyst who understood their meaning according to principles of unconscious communication, such as symbolism. Patients tended to be more refractory to these interpretations. The analyst's focus turned first to an arduous struggle with the inherent nature of resistance to revelation, subsequently to a working through of the significance of the revelation as understood by the analyst, and eventually, once insight was obtained, to the patient's making changes. The difficulties encountered by the analyst were explained by adhesive libido, repetition compulsion, a need for punishment based on unconscious guilt, or countertransference interferences. In retrospect, during a period when analyst-patient communication was based on relatively fixed formulations of intrapsychic structural conflict, the analyst "knew" the unconscious determinants and a spirit of inquiry was often lacking.

In this book we will examine communication broadly from a developmental perspective and more narrowly from the perspective of clinical psychoanalysis. We propose that all exchanges, negotiations, and conflicts that children or adults have with others or with themselves can be illuminated as aspects of the success or failure of communication. Further, we propose that all communications in analysis whether about physiological regulation, attachment, exploration, sexuality, or aversiveness require an underlying persistent spirit of inquiry to give the therapeutic enterprise its guiding purpose.

Unlike direct questioning and probing, a spirit of inquiry is a guiding attitude, a world view that unites analysts across a spectrum of theories. A spirit of inquiry establishes an ambiance that persists when direct exploratory efforts are prevented by enactments and overwhelming affect states. A spirit of inquiry provides vitality to the psychoanalytic search for subjective and intersubjective awareness. Empathic perception is not necessarily positive, salutary, or directional. We can "sense into" the experiential world of patients not only to help them but also to know how to exploit, manipulate, seduce, or infantilize them. Even when empathic perception by analysts is used to sense how to relate beneficially to patients and at times form highly meaningful attachments, we believe that psychoanalysis is intimacy formed in a spirit of inquiry rather than intimacy itself. In our prior writings about motivation, we have called attention to the diverse voices emanating from five self-organizing and self-stabilizing systems. We have described the verbal affective messages that can alert analyst and analysand to what system is dominant, active, or dormant.

New questions point today's analysts in the direction of communication. How do we communicate with ourselves? Without a reasonably open source of self-knowledge, neither patient nor analyst can "free associate." What facilitates openness to self-awareness on the part of patient and analyst? And most salient, how does each influence the other?

In asking, How do we communicate with *ourselves?* Our attention is immediately directed to the nature of *self* and to *identity*. As long as the pioneering analysts dealt with the symptomotology of adults, selfhood and identity could be treated as "givens." Once childhood, especially the infant and toddler periods, became a subject of analytic inquiry, questions about the development of self and identity became germane to theorists such as Spitz, Erikson, Sullivan, Mahler, and Lichtenstein. Similar questions began to be asked about adolescents by Anna Freud, Erikson, Blos, and others. Additional questions evolved from the failure to thrive of hospitalized orphans observed by Spitz and Provence and the children separated from their families during war observed by Anna Freud. What is needed to sustain life and to assure well balanced development? What is the nature of caregiver-child interdependence? Combining these two strands Kohut asked how does a healthy sense of self develop, how is it maintained, what in the interdependent flow of life disturbs it?

Theorizing about the role of emotion in the organization of the sense of self and identity shifted analytic attention from strangulated affect as central to symptom formation, to derivatives of drives, and then to emotion as an increasingly salient feature of both personal experience and relationships with others. As attention shifted to emotion or affect (Tomkins, Emde, Krystal), relational perspectives and self psychology expanded and competed with Freudian and Kleinian views as explanatory concepts for psychoanalysis. The focus then expanded from psychic structure to interactively coconstructed, lived experience. In this evolution, interdependence and interpersonal relations became intersubjectivity; how we separate and individuate became how we operate in a matrix in which we are constantly oscillating between experiences that allow us to feel close and supported, and experiences that trigger aversiveness, even alienation. At the same time, the "empirical infant" challenged the "clinical infant" (Stern, 1985).

The vulnerability of the (clinical) infant had been exaggerated in concepts such as birth trauma (Rank), death instinct (Klein), orgasmic distress (Mahler), primal anxiety (Sullivan). In contrast, Kohut, closer in his theorizing to the infant conceived by empirical research, described the infant as strong, meaning that the neonate is born with innate responses to the ecological niche of a "good enough" caregiver-infant matrix. Self psychology identifies the source of the strength as arising from the interaction between the empathic capacity of the caregiver to recognize the needs of the growing developing infant and the robustness of the infant's signals.

Empathic perception, the sensing by one person (a perceiver) into the experiential world of another (the perceived), implies three aspects of communication. First, that messages are being communicated internally in the perceived one. The perceived one has experiential states as varied as the drowsiness of a baby or the complex symbolic message of the dream in an adult. Second, some approximation of the perceived one's communication to herself is able to be communicated to the perceiver, that is the caregiver is able to decipher the communicative signs of drowsiness or the analyst may understand the theme of a dream narrative. Third, the attended, intercommunicated information is absorbed in a manner that the perceiver can communicate knowingly to herself, that is the caregiver can tell herself the baby is sleepy or the analyst can formulate the meanings expressed in the dream.

The ecological niche of infant-caregiver has developed from an evolutionary leap that permits communication to take place in two modes. Infants can communicate with themselves and their caregivers through sensations, affects, and gestures. Adults retain this mode of communication but have the additional mode of symbolic, especially verbal, usage. Growing children make an evolutionary leap into the duality of nonverbal and verbal modes. They are enabled to be expressive in verbal and nonverbal modes through the communication to them of a process taking place about, for, and with them in the experiential world of their caregivers. Stated differently, infants already exist in maps or stories about them in their caregivers' experiential world before they move into being uniquely, symbolically aware selves (with name, identity, and characterological features). The who-she-is and who-she-is-to-become involves a continuous process of intercommunication that is augmented greatly by the development of the unique human capacity for speech.

Listening, sensing into, decoding, and deciphering motivation-driven messages is of course not confined to analysis. Such attendance on messages occurs not only in all conversational exchanges but also when reflecting on one's own messages. Decoding and deciphering meaning from another (and one's self) are themselves motivated, that is, to fulfill a conscious or unconscious expectation. We have mantained that along with such well recognized sources of motivation as the need for physiological requirements, attachments, sensual pleasure and sexual excitement, and the means to respond aversively through antagonism and withdrawal, the need to explore one's environment and assert one's preferences within it constitute an independent system of motivation. In its infantile expression, exploratory-assertive motivations are best observed in "pure" form when a fed, well-tended, and talked to baby is placed in a play table or seat and scans with obvious interest all the moving or stable objects in her surround. She will look longer at those she prefers or can manipulate, expressing a preference for active influence on the environment rather than passive observing. In its adult expression we might think of the whole process of scientific conceptualization, study, and research. The animating affects in infant and adult are interest, curiosity, and working to achieve a feeling of efficacy and competence, with varied levels of playfulness. During analysis, at a given moment, exploration may be the dominant motive of the analyst or the analysand, or both. The subject of the exploration may be messages derived from any of the motivational systems including the exploratory-assertive.

An analyst may encourage a patient to be curious about his choice of his professional interest. But so might a career counselor, so what is the difference? Likewise, a man becoming seriously interested in a woman may inquire how does she feel about him and try to get a better understanding of their attachment. So what is the difference, since how do you feel about me (and all the past variants of me) is an almost constant, implied or overt, question of analyst and patient about each other? The analytic exchange is unique in that analyst and analysand have moments when they are like the scientist seriously asking meaningful questions. They have moments like the child playing with a toy as they play with an image in a dream. They have moments like lovers who have suspended thinking about love to experience fully their feelings. There are moments like enemies who have suspended rationality to experience more fully their angry feelings. And moments during which their hunger or physical pain or drowsiness overwhelm any exploratory intent. Thus, during analysis, the immediacy of exploration *may* be manifest or suspended. It *must* be suspended at moments for the experiential intensity of interactions, enactments, and engagements to occur. Consequently, during analysis, interactions, enactments, and engagements have the potential to transform analysis into an intimate relationship like any other intimate relationship or a battle ground like any other battle ground, or a cry for relief of painful physiological or affective states like any medical-psychiatric approach.

Accordingly, an underlying sense of purpose must be present or easily recoverable to sustain analysis as a search for expansion of personal meaning. We regard this sustaining underlying sense of purpose to be a spirit of inquiry. When an analysis is threatened by the loss of intention represented by dominance of intimacy for the sake of intimacy, or battle, or symptom relief, or sterile intellectual exploration, the underlying spirit of inquiry

rebounds into the intersubjective field acting like a compass setting helping to reset the voyage of discovery on its course.

Not only does a spirit of inquiry protect the purpose of analysis, but it ensures the open-mindedness needed for a search for
personal meaning. Exploration in analysis as we construe it is built
on the value of inquiry itself. Inquiry-based analysis is value free
as to what motivation is explored and what communication is
responded to. As we stated in our previous proposals, we consider the exploratory motivational system to be a distinct system.
Now we wish to emphasize that exploration as a search for novelty and efficacy is present in all motivational systems. The over-
lapping of exploration across motivational systems facilitates the
integration of all motivation into a cohesive sense of self. Stated
differently, the inclusion of exploratory motives in maps associated with activities in each system increases reentrant possibilities
(see chapters 1 and 2). Thus, a spirit of inquiry helps to maintain
the stability of analytic purpose and promotes integration of aspects
of each motivational thrust. As analysands develop their own spirit
of inquiry, the overlap of this sense of purpose gives to communication during moments in analysis an ease of flow, sometimes
even a commonality of words, thoughts and feelings.

The spirit of inquiry is critical for addressing one of the most
persistent paradoxes during analysis. Patients (and analysts as well)
have a deep desire to be known, recognized, and appreciated for
who they truly are. At the same time, no patient (and no analyst)
escapes a desire to protect the privacy, the secret, of some aspect
of self, conscious or unconscious, that is associated with shame,
humiliation, embarrassment, or guilt. Traditionally psychoanalysis has privileged investigation of the wish not to be known. Self
psychology has given greater emphasis to the wish to achieve
recognition through being listened to empathically. The spirit of
inquiry assures the flexibility for the analyst's attentional focus to
shift, permitting the patient to experience himself as known while
the desire for privacy and deception is equally known. Exploration
additionally includes the patient's need to know who the analyst
is and the analyst's appropriate boundary for revelation. As
analysands join in the spirit of inquiry, the same attentional shift

between learning about himself through introspection and the search for the identity of the analyst provides a maximally desirable mutuality to the analytic endeavor.

Ideally, the intersubjective realm of an analysis is imbued by a spirit of inquiry of both participants. Often this ideal is not achieved. Sometimes when patients experience altered affective states such as depression (see chapter 6), euphoria, rage, withdrawal, dissociation, shame, and panic, a spirit of inquiry is absent. Especially when prolonged, the analyst must rely on his intimacy with himself, his introspection, and what empathic glimmers the patient permits to maintain a spirit of inquiry under the difficult circumstances.

Throughout our discussion of communication in psychoanalysis, we will be cognizant of three perspectives: historical changes in theoretical focus, the subjectivity of the analyst, and the complexity of intersubjectivity.

Here is Teicholz (1999) on historic change:

> When we approach a discussion of what the analyst says and does, how she conceptualizes the analytic relationship, and what her basic attitudes toward the patient and the work are, the differences between older and newer theories take on greater significance. For instance, in turning from Freud's almost exclusive focus on interpretation and insight, Kohut and Loewald, independent of one another, introduced the notion that the analyst must convey an attitude that provides the patient with essential developmental experiences and must be available for aspects of relationship required for psychic growth [p. 242].

We will demonstrate that intimate communication in an analysis conducted with a spirit of inquiry facilitates a relationship required for both psychic growth and understanding.

Schwaber (1998) states her view of the analyst's subjectivity:

> "My advocacy" is of the sustained, painful, often jarring pursuit of seeing ourselves, our values and assumptions, through the patient's eyes, often initially unconscious to

her, or resisted by her, a reflection we may not have in awareness otherwise, and a perspective on transference (still expressing the past but) behind which we cannot hide. . . . I do not forego my own vantage point, nor can I listen without a theoretical base; I do not seek to empathize as such, but to invite often rigorous reflection; I must draw upon my separate view to guide me to what may be hidden in hers [p. 26].

Schwaber's elegant statement points to the need for analysts' self-communication and to the need for them to be on intimate and self-accepting terms with the discoveries about their patients and especially about themselves that emerge from self-inquiry and self-reflection. To apprehend the patient's meaning requires such flexible shifting of focus.

Meares (2000) says about the complexity of intersubjectivity:

Conversation is the result of an interplay between two minds whose words begin to create a third zone which was not previously extant and which would not have arisen but through the activity of the single minds alone. The therapist, as participant, cannot without breaking up this shared creation, suddenly take a role in which he or she is the objective observer of the patient as subject. This new subject-object form of relationship is discontinuous with the conversational flow, like the emergence of traumatic memory. What the "objective observer" says by way of interpretation does not work since it is in a zone of experience split off from that of the stream of consciousness.

Yet, at the same time, the therapist must be an observer. He or she has to play out a paradox. He or she must stay within the intersubjective experience and at the same time become aware of the shifts in the patient's, as well as his or her own, states and behaviors. . . .

The double stance of the therapist, who is both participant and observer of the conversational experience, leads, in ideal circumstance, to an exploration and representation of the "minute particulars" which show the unconscious

determination of certain aspect of the therapeutic conversation [p. 138].

In our clinical examples we illustrate both the context and the
spirit of inquiry through which the meanings of the minute particulars of analytic conversations are opened.

As the dichotomy between drive theory and relational theory
became crystallized (Greenberg and Mitchell, 1983), a tilt toward
the "relational" became manifest in many guises: the self–selfobject
matrix, interpersonal relationships, attachment theory, object relations, and intersubjectivity. While we champion this trend, we
believe that human subjectivity and intersubjectivity cannot be
accounted for without an adequate theory of motivation and communication. Attachment theory, through its robust integration
of strange situation strategies and the linguistic analyses of the
Adult Attachment Interview, provides overwhelmingly convincing evidence for the link between crucial relationships and communication. Finally, we hope to demonstrate that a contemporary
psychoanalysis involves a relationship that permits an inquiry in
its nature, the motivations that rise and fall, and the modes of
communication that reveal and conceal the subjectivity and intersubjectivity that evolves.

CHAPTER ONE

HOW DO WE EXPLAIN THE DEVELOPMENT OF COMMUNICATION WITH SELF AND OTHER IN INFANCY? PART 1

Our purpose is to offer clinicians a way to reconceptualize both the significance hitherto given to verbal associations and insight, and the importance now given to empathy and relational interaction. Communication is in our view the overarching phenomenon that integrates the verbal and nonverbal features of analytic therapy. By communication we mean exchanges of explicit and implicit information interpersonally and to one's self. The main body of the book details our view of communication during treatment. But first we will take up communication during infancy. Communication is an integral part of the developing child's intersubjective world long before the symbolic meaning of words are the shared currency of caregiver-infant informational exchanges. In the first two chapters we describe the origin of the development of communication before and after symbol sharing. We will emphasize a two-way stream of communication balanced between attentiveness to inner self and attentiveness to others.

We will draw on our prior writings (Lichtenberg, 1989; Lichtenberg, Lachmann, and Fosshage, 1992, 1996) in which we proposed five motivational systems. Each motivational system develops in response to an innate need and each involves caregiver's responses. The five motivational systems self-organize and self-stabilize in response to the need for (1) regulation of physiological requirements; (2) attachment to individuals and affiliation to groups; (3) exploration and the assertion of preferences; (4) aversive reactions of antagonism and withdrawal; and (5) sensual enjoyment and sexual excitement. Between each system and within each system dialectic tensions exist so that the dominance of experience by a particular system is in constant flux in response to changes in context and intersubjective pressures. Hierarchical rearrangement within developing systems is a constant feature. This feature of motivational systems, their potential for hierarchial alteration, is particularly important to our presentation in chapters 1 and 2 of the development of communication and in subsequent chapters in the portrayal of change during psychoanalytic therapies conducted in a spirit of inquiry.

Throughout the book we make frequent references to attachment research and theory. We refer to the categories established through the Strange Situation Test. Based on the SST, researchers have identified specific strategies infants utilize to ensure a stable base of safety. One strategy played out between child and caregiver ensures a secure attachment. Other strategies of anxious-resisting and avoidance serve to maintain an insecure attachment. In some instances, any of these strategies prove unworkable and for periods of time infants will lapse into stages of disorganization, disorientation, and even dissociation. Adults have also been tested by an attachment interview, the AAI, as to their state of mind with respect to their attachment experiences. The groupings are those whose state of mind with respect to attachment are autonomous and secure, those that are preoccupied and those that are dismissive. In addition there are those who by virtue of being unresolved to loss and trauma suffer lapses in coherence, disorientation, and dissociation (see *Psychoanalytic Inquiry*, 1989, Vol. 19, No. 4: Attachment Research and Psychoanalysis: Theoretical Considerations, and No. 5: Clinical Implications).

We hold to a bidirectional, interactional systems view of communication. At times we may emphasize: (1) the child's (or patient's) communicative contribution as a self-regulating system; and (2) the caregiver's (or therapist's) communications as a self-regulating system ideally guided by empathic responsiveness and a spirit of provision (or inquiry). But neither system can be described without reference to (3) the parent-child (therapist-patient) dyad as an interactive communicative field—a uniquely organized system of its own (see Beebe and Lachmann, 2002).

After the developmental chapters, we will reframe familiar and current concepts of therapy by considering psychoanalysis as a process of communication conducted in a spirit of inquiry.

Part 1: The Emergence of a Communicative Self (0 to 18 Months)

As living organisms, we are dependent on nutritional-expulsion exchanges. As primates we are dependent on relational exchanges. As humans we are dependent on informational exchanges that facilitate communication with others and especially with ourselves. Why especially with ourselves? Probably alone of primates, humans have a stream of consciousness that, after the development of symbolization, allows us to converse with ourselves. From an early age, our experience involves a continuous interplay between discourse with others and discourse with ourselves. Communication is enlivened by affects triggered by perception of the external and inner world. The interplay of our experience affects what we can know about ourselves and how we feel about it. To be intimate with others is a widely recognized goal of human development. Less well recognized as a primary goal is to be intimate with oneself. What can we sense about ourselves, our feelings, sensations, thoughts, intentions, our view of others and our view of the view others have of us? Does our sense of self allow us to live within our skin more or less contentedly and productively? Along with empathic sensitivity, a cohesive sense of self, intersubjectivity, and systems of motivation, communication offers a perspective that is necessary to feel our way into how intimacy with others and with one's self develops.

Affects and sensations are basic to a sense of familiarity with oneself and to the mode of consciousness of infancy. The uniquely human level of post-infancy consciousness depends on a symbolic realm mediated through words, images, and metaphor integrated with affect and sensation. The symbolic processing of information is fundamental to the stream of internal monologue-dialogue that characterizes communication with oneself and accompanies speech to others. Communication, however, including parent's speech from birth (and before), is interwoven in all caregiver-infant exchanges long before symbolic processing by the baby is possible. Talking with and to a baby not only consolidates attachment but also builds intuitive communicative capacities prior to words themselves becoming the medium for the exchange of meaning. Growing infants are held in their caregivers' symbolic world before they form one of their own. Caregivers ease their infants into a symbolic world of inner and outer communication by conveying their recognition of their particular baby through the flow of their "chatter" to and with the baby. Failure to communicate the recognition of a baby's humanness (subjectivity) and essential uniqueness will impair the development of that baby's attachment and other motivational systems and its sense of self.

Various essential provisions need to evolve from the explicit and implicit regulation of caregiver and infant. Attachment research has documented a sense of safety as the caregiver provides a secure base at times of danger and loss (Bowlby, 1969, 1973, 1980; Main, 2000). Self psychology and motivational systems theory have described the sensitive balancing of needs of each partner across a spectrum of motivational systems (Lichtenberg, 1989).

Concomitant with a view of a sense of self evolving out of the dynamics of infant-caregiver interactions, modern neurophysiology envisions the brain's evolving out of the constant mutual influence of an innate adaptive potential and the environment. Edelman (1987, 1992) posits the brain developing before birth as a process of neuronal selection guided by genetic instructions. During fetal development, neurons and neuronal groups migrate in unpredictable ways to form unique patterns of cortical circuitry. After birth a second selection begins, guided by basic biases (values) that are experienced as feelings. After birth very little is pre-programmed; mostly the brain creates itself through a dynamic interaction with the environment. Gone are static views of structures formed fixedly, functions tightly localized, and simple restraints like feedback homeostatic control. Theorists such as Edelman and Damasio (1999) describe a brain that has both stability and extraordinary plasticity enabling it to undergo self-organization and emergent order with every lived experience. Memory is no longer encoded or deposited in the brain and reactivated in photographic fixity, but is initially selected by bias and is context-dependent in its recall. Perception and sensation are not simply recordings of the external and internal worlds but are acts of creation made through categorization and mapping. Maps are not merely laid down as functional tracks but are constantly reformed and recategorized. A continuous communication, characterized by Edelman as reentrant signaling, connects the active maps. As individuals organize their own categories, maps, and reentrant signals, a world of personal meaning and reference is constructed.

Consciousness is created in two momentous steps. The linking of very early memory maps with a current perception creates primary (Edelman) or core (Damasio) consciousness—a state of being mentally aware of things in the world in the form of here-and-now lived experience. The second step, a linking of symbolic memory, linguistically organized concepts, and a representation of self, creates higher-order consciousness. In higher-order (Edelman) or extended (Damasio) consciousness, concepts of self, past, and future can be connected to here and now awareness. Consciousness of consciousness, and reflective recognition of cognitive affective intentional states becomes possible. The complex picture of a brain creating an ever-changing individualistic picture of a world full of personal meaning coincides with our sense of a self experiencing an integrated and orchestrated stream of consciousness. Overall these theories postulate continuous communication within the brain in linkage with internal and external perception.

An Emergent Sense of Self (0–2 Months)

Neonates can be viewed as setting up an ecological niche in which they recreate conditions that enable them to experience familiar states by which they recognize themselves (Sander, 1983). How can we envision the emergent sense of neonates becoming familiar with themselves? The caregiver's contribution to the ecological niche lies in empathic recognition of and response to the infant's internally derived needs. The infant's contribution lies in being able to offer recognizable signals of need and to activate specific innate and learned response patterns that permit the caregiver's responses to be effective. An example is an infant's cry that her mother correctly reads as hunger and institutes holding and feeding. The infant's experience would combine an internal sensation of discomfort with a generalized feeling of distress, the activation of sucking with rhythmical rate changes, followed by the relief of distress and sensations leading to an internal sensation of fullness. The internal sensation of fullness may become distress from abdominal distention requiring relief by burping. The release of air may be followed by more intake to a point of satiety, disinterest in sucking, and conclude with rejection of the nipple. The mother's experience is one of efficacy in her ministrations and the recognition of the particularities of her baby at that time. She is apt to express this as: "Oh, you were really hungry. OK I'm here. Oh, you need to be burped. OK now. Well you really have slowed down. I guess you've had enough." The inevitable repetitions of this shared response pattern creates for the baby an experience of changing affect states. The changing affect states combine bodily sensations of internal and generalized distress, supportive holding and positioning, internal fullness and generalized relief, perceptions of mother's face, eye contact, and her spoken voice. We are aware that our description implies more linearity than is appropriate for the complex interactive system of mutual influence in continuous operation between infant and caregiver.

A "package" of changing internal affect-laden state changes and external tactile, visual, olfactory, and auditory perceptions repeated with the same person or similarly enough with more than one caregiver becomes for the neonate a familiar re-creation, a memory map, a presymbolic nonverbal story (Damasio, 1999) or "scene" (Edelman, 1992) that we believe is experienced as an emergent sense of self. Bucci offers a similar accounting: "The chunking of continuous representations into prototypic images based on equivalence of structure, or function, or association in time and place may occur across as well as within modalities . . .

(forming) . . . prototypic episodes. . . . Repeated episodes provide the basis for the construction of . . . emotion schemas, from
the beginning of life, well prior to the acquisition of language,
and also determine the process by which emotional experience
may be symbolized and communicated to other" (1997, p. 183).
Of course, feeding is but one of many repeated interactions that
have a feeling story to be remembered and re-created—elimi-
nating and being diapered, being put to sleep, being conversed
with and stimulated pleasurably during alert periods of comfort,
being soothed at times of nonspecific fussiness, being held, fon-
dled, kissed, tussled about, being left without direct intrusion to
explore crib, toy, or a button on mother's blouse.

The terms "emergent" and "re-create" require further elaboration. To conceive of an infant as capable of the experience of
re-creating implies several innate abilities. In experiments, infants
have been found to change their sucking rhythm or turn their
heads a set number of times to one side (Papousek and Papousek,
1975) in order to turn on a light display they are preprogrammed
to enjoy ("value," Edelman). The infants will continue to do this
much longer if they are the agent than if the light is turned on
for them or randomly activated. In conversational runs with their
mother, infants will activate responses when their mother pauses
or is distracted. We assume the infants have a primitive form of
agency—I do it, I start it, I create it, and, now that it is repeated,
I re-create it. Only what marks the re-creation for the infant? We
believe the "actions" become meaningful as affect-sensory experiences—interest, a sense of efficacy, and competence in the
exploratory activities, and joy of intimacy eventuating in the
enlivening smile and body jiggling. In Damasio's view, these
actions produce such changes that the organism has a "feeling"
of knowing about, that is, the infant has a feeling that he can
sense that he is feeling.

Emergent has a double meaning: awareness begins and I
become aware. We can draw an analogy to awakening in a strange
room. First, light enters your eyes and next you are aware of the
change from sleep state, more what has happened than what you
have done. Then you feel the stuffed sensation in your nose and

remember you have a cold, so it is you who is awakening. But, with some anxiety, where? You scan your surroundings, place yourself in your friend's house, and take mental charge of your emergence into the day ahead. Using a similar construct, Damasio (1999) states that "stepping into the light is also a powerful metaphor for consciousness, for the birth of the knowing mind, for the simple and yet momentous coming of the sense of self into the world of the mental" (p. 3). Thus we can say we re-create our self each day that we metaphorically step into awakeness or after any major affective state change, as from a fright to a state of calm. This is not in accord with the Cartesian formula "I know therefore I am," but is rather a matter of I *feel* and I sense I feel right now, therefore I am I. This here-and-now-I-am emerges into being with core consciousness. The core consciousness of self precedes higher consciousness and language organized thought when the child can reflectively recognize and monitor thoughts, feelings, plans, and prior actions.

For this explanation of an emergent sense of self to be credible, the central nervous system must have a number of complex capacities present at or very shortly after birth. Lived experience in the form of core consciousness involves perception, categorization, and mapping. Similar repeated sequences must be generalized and recategorized, and simple contingent or causal links established. Moreover, recognition of changes of affect states must be appreciated as a process that is occurring for a sense of creating and re-creating to evolve. The repeated experience and the sense of re-creating activates an elemental consciousness that is both flowing and differentiated in the here and now. Categorization, generalization, and recategorization are responsible for the organization of discrete states into feeling stories or affect schemas. However, much lived experience and communication occurs as a continuous flow (Fogel, 1993; Knoblauch, 1996, 2000) of nonverbal contours of vocal and breathing volume, rhythm, tempo, and tone, and of gestural patterning, proprioceptive shifts of face and body, body gurgles, smells, and expulsions. In caregiver-infant exchanges these continuous processes have a background influence on the essential affect tonality mapped into the more discrete feeling stories. Their ephemeral micromoments and bidirectional flow give to both early and later communication a basic pattern of being shaped by loosely formulated nonverbal cues that flow along with later exchanges of verbalized symbolic meanings.

Damasio (1999) proposes a theory of the development of elemental consciousness that coincides to a degree with the view we espouse:

> As the brain forms images of an object—such as a face, a melody, a toothache, the memory of an event—and as the images of the object affect the state of the organism, yet another level of brain structure creates a swift nonverbal account of the events that are taking place in the varied brain regions activated as a consequence of the object-organism interaction. The mapping of the object-related consequences occurs in first-order neural maps representing proto-self and object; the account of the *causal relationship* between object and organism can only be captured in second-order neural maps. . . . . [W]ith the license of metaphor, one might say that the swift second-order nonverbal account narrates a story: *that of the organism caught in the act of representing its own changing state as it goes about representing something else.* But the astonishing fact is that the knowable entity of the catcher has been created in the narrative of the creative process [p. 110].

Damasio equates core consciousness with the narrative account formed in a near-infinite series of pulses as we navigate the world. He cites the hippocampus, brain stem, and insula as the brain structures most involved in the detailed making and unmaking of neural maps or representations of the total physical state. The non-conscious foundation of self that Damasio calls "protoself" arises from the collective maps forming and altering a response to encounters requiring homeostatic adjustment. The essence of the core self is the representation in a second order map of the protoself being modified. "Because of the permanent availability of provoking objects, it [core consciousness] is continuously generated and thus appears continuous in time" (p. 175). The wellspring of consciousness is not language but the feeling of knowing that we have feelings.

Returning to psychological observation, affects prime the neonate to activate innate and learned responses to anything that alleviates an aversive state or augments a positive state. The infant is thus motivated to connect antecedents and consequences, that is, to learn incrementally (Tomkins, 1962, 1963). The intrapsychic development of a sense of self is inextricably context related or, in Kohut's terms, the baby's self is strong because it is embedded in a self-selfobject matrix. I would add that the self can only be construed as "strong" if (1) the sense of self develops as an affective being who has been responded to by an animated empathically sensitive caregiver ready to initiate needed provision and, (2) the sense of self includes a conviction of being able to initiate affective, need-fulfilling responses from the caregiver. The baby's growing sense of an elementary I-ness through the re-creation of affective experience combined with a recognition of being able to trigger affective need-fulfilling responses from the caregiver (a we-ness) fills out Kohut's definition of self as a center of initiative.

The sensitivity of the communication of affective state between caregiver and neonate can be appreciated through the study of both pairs who are successfully able to bring about secure attachment (Katie, our second example) and pairs in which insecure attachment (Main, 2000) occurs even in this early period, as in the case of Kierra.

Kierra

One of us (JL) was asked by a research group to evaluate the videotapes of a bottle feeding of 18-day-old Kierra by her 16-year-old mother in a facility for single first-time mothers who had no other support. I evaluated the feeding as effective in nutrient transmission and ordinary in maternal attentiveness although the mother was essentially silent throughout. I next viewed a feeding at one month 22 days in which Kierra was fully head and eye averted from her silent mother, who appeared both unaware and unconcerned. The researchers told me they had reviewed the tapes repeatedly before discovering a clue to how in the 18-day feeding the mother was communicating to Kierra that while she was conscientiously performing the task of feeding, she was not enacting or creating an intersubjective experience with the baby. While she held Kierra firmly enough and positioned the bottle well with her right arm and hand, her left hand was limp with a small space between her hand and the baby's body. Further while her eyes were focused attentively, it was not clear that she was observing the baby. The mother had been told to burp the baby when the bottle reached a mark so it is probable that the silent young mother was more attentive to the bottle than Kierra. At the 1-month 22-day feeding the left hand was completely detached from any connection to Kierra.

A bath scene at 18 days strongly suggested that Kierra's mother was relating to her as an inanimate object whom or which she had to service. Kierra's whole body was scrubbed vigorously by the silent 16-year-old who, in her determination to do what she was instructed to do, appeared to be oblivious of the child's continuous loud crying. Kierra's crying is so painful to audiences who hear the tape that they recoil long before the two-minute sequence is complete.

At nine months, a play sequence with her mother reveals a stationary depressed child neatly dressed who doesn't crawl or demonstrate any interest in toys. At 18 months, during the initial part of a feeding, Kierra is attentive to the video and not her mother. Then, for a brief moment, the two make contact as Kierra offers her mother a marshmallow. This sequence shows Kierra being able to develop a degree of attachment through a reversal of caregiving. At 24 months, in an outdoor play sequence, Kierra signaled her desire to be picked up while her mother wanted to continue to play with the toys.

As the patterns of being cared for by her young mother became repetitive, what affects can we use our empathy to imagine Kierra re-created, forming the origins of her emergent sense of self? On the positive side Kierra could come to experience that a re-creation of a sensation of hunger and the affect of distress would lead to sucking, nutrient intake, relief, and satiety. This positive re-creation would result in a degree of homeostatic stability in her nonconscious protoself and a conscious sense of core self as a successful initiator in this significant repeated pattern of physiological regulation. Successful initiation of signals to be fed can serve as the basis for a reversal into feeding another in play with dolls or as observed later in her feeding of her mother, their most effective moment of mutual attachment intimacy. The premise behind this finding is that all patterns are formed in their neural pathways as dualities of self and other, as done to and doer, recipient or agent (Beebe, Lachmann, and Jaffe, 1997). We can also recognize a positive side to Kierra's mother's persistence as caregiver, thereby creating the core sense of familiarity with the affects triggered by her appearance, smell, sound, and touch. As attachment research has indicated, infant and mother will form a strategy for their essential connection even if its form is insecure. Insecure is more than a categorical designation, however, it is an affect—the opposite of a sense of safety. The sense of insecurity, repeated in every feeding, every bathing, every joyless episode of play, is a powerful communication from mother to child. The message is: I can't or don't hold you in a manner to prevent your feeling unsupported. I can't touch your skin so you feel sensually embraced. I can't bathe you in my affectionate informative chatter because I can only communicate my dulled silence, the deadness of what I can internally communicate with myself. Without my or your knowing how it came about, you will re-create a depressive avoidant deadness as your frequent response to me, yourself, and others. By one month and 22 days, Kierra is saying in actions, I can re-create a more satisfying core consciousness by looking off into the room or at the man with the camera than by looking at your immobile face. Since you don't seem to notice, we can fall into this mutual, detached attachment as a given of our life together.

The Developing Core Sense of Self (2 to 8 Months)

Katie, the 14½-week-old first child of a sensitive middle-class married mother is seen sitting at a feeding table. The videotape made in the course of family life by the father has been used as a research control indicating secure attachment. As her mother fills a spoon with a gooey white substance, Katie moves her hands from her face holding her arms and hands up at her side. In synchrony with the spoon's arrival Katie opens her mouth and as the spoon is withdrawn she moves her hands to her face to push at the residue all over her mouth. This is repeated a number of times with an occasional face wipe with a cloth by her mother who chats with Katie periodically. If Katie is not ready, mother pauses and goes forward or withdraws the spoon. If mother is not ready, Katie does not take the arms extended position. At one point Katie's father introjects a teasing remark about how much they like their new house, and Katie's mother turns to make a sardonic retort so that both parents have withdrawn their attention from Katie. Viewed in slow motion, Katie can be seen to turn her gaze away, droop her head, and slump her posture. Her appearance in the split screen is one of sadness. This whole sequence occupies about 30 seconds. As Katie's mother refocuses on her, Katie is instantly revitalized and they immediately resume their well-choreographed dancelike interplay. Finally, Katie indicates a beginning loss of interest in the food, switches to controlling the spoon herself, and then stops. Mother states, "Oh you've had enough," offers a bottle which Katie refuses, ending the feeding sequence. At 9 months Katie, seated at the same feeding table, is picking up Cheerios with interest and happily feeding herself.

When looked at from a variety of sequences—bathing, feeding, play, "conversations," hugging, kissing, and upset moments—the tapes of Katie and her mother and father demonstrate the communicative power of affective attunement. In the course of making constant adjustment to the affective and gestural signals of the other, mother, child, and father establish a rhythmic relatedness that raises or lowers thresholds of arousal. Looked at behaviorally, correct affect and gestural appreciation smoothes the way for physiological regulation, attachment intimacy, exploratory play and assertiveness, rapid recovery from aversive states, and sensual enjoyment. Looked at as a form of communication, correct affect and gestural appreciation establishes the infant's core sense of self through the recognition of her individuality and her connection to her particular parents. Katie becomes Katie as her mother and father establish "I know you—you like to eat slowly and be talked to and play in the water, and—and you belong to this mother and this father—and we belong to you." Attunement, mutual responsiveness, and communication lead to neural pathways, what Damasio calls "stories" of Katie in this or that activity. The sets of neural pathways bearing on these exchanges, those of Katie's and those of her mother's and father's, will coincide more or less well. In Katie's psyche, the core sense of self is one of core consciousness of her identity in shifting motivational states with words as a familiar perceptual and categorical component of herself being with others but as yet without symbolic meaning. In her parents' psyche Katie has a verbally organized biographic self that is being interwoven into their individual and collective (family) biographic senses of self. Eventually as Katie forms her own symbolically organized biographic self from her remembered lived experiences, her sense of who she is will coincide more or less well with the biographic self preconceived for her—preparation for a "true" self (Winnicott, 1960) as her securely attached core self would predict.

Our understanding of attunement—to bring into harmony—has been greatly enhanced by research on mother-infant interaction. Stern (1985) described the cross-modal responsiveness by which a mother watching an infant at play waving a block will hum, head wag, hand gesture, or foot tap in a matching rhythm and intensity. Recent studies by Jaffe et al. (1999) on vocal exchanges further advance our knowledge of attunement. They confirm that "proto-conversational rhythmic coordination of sound and silence is important in conveying emotional information prior to speech onset" and that "coordinated interpersonal timing is an early communication system in infancy and constitutes a scaffolding for infant social development." In their research, the process central to attunement shifts from matching to tracking. Contrary to the expectation that a high coordination of maternal tracking of an infant's communication was optimal, the researchers found that too high a degree of coordination represented a hypervigilent form of mutual influence. We propose that excessive coordination would be experienced by the infant as intrusive, a primitive form of entrapment (Meares, 2000). A high level of coordination, especially as it played out under stress with a stranger, was predictive of anxious-resistant or disorganized/disoriented attachments. Optimal coordination in interpersonal tuning lay in the middle range and was predictive of secure attachment at one year. They note a striking parallel to research on rhythmic communication between neural networks in the forebrain, where a midrange degree of coordination correlated with maximal transmission of information. Midrange in practice means "slow down, follow the baby slowly, repeat but slightly vary sounds or expressions, 'cool it' when the baby facially dampens or looks away, and generally stay with baby's arousal level (without ever topping it)."

Alternatively, insufficient coordination with the infant's vocal rhythms is devitalizing, a predicter of an avoidant insecure attachment. At four months, coordination of interpersonal timing is not a fixed phenomenon. It varies with whether it is with a familiar person or a stranger in a familiar place such as the house or an unfamiliar laboratory. The variance of response attests to the complexity of the four-month-old's social capacity. At one year of age, dialogic vocal rhythms are predictive of social interactions. The Jaffe, Beebe group see the varying rhythmic patterns as social procedures for managing attention, activity level, turntaking, joining, interruption, yielding, and tracking. Operant as procedural memories, infants and toddlers use these patterns to coordinate with adults and to respond to novelty and challenge.

Communication during the first year has also been studied in the triangular form of mother, father, and infant (Fivaz-Depeursinge and Corboz-Warnery, 1999). Using an experimental design with the three participants seated in an equilateral triangle, observations were based on how well the family system worked to sustain play and make transitions. Four sequences and three transitions were required: first, one parent plays with the child, the other observes; second, a transition to the other parent playing, the first observing; then, a transition to all three involved in play, and finally, a transition to the parents being primarily involved with each other. Observations began at three months and continued at intervals during the first year of the baby's life. The experimenters observed the movements of the pelvis, torso, gazes, and facial expressions. Were baby and each parent participating in the assigned goal? Were they maintaining focal attention, guiding their interactions with each other? Were they able to organize a way to make the transitions and sustain play? Were they maintaining focal attention, building up their interactions with each other? Were they picking up and responding to each other's affective signals? "The terms that capture the different qualities of the family alliances are *cooperation, stress, collusion, and disorder*" (p. 9). In cooperation, liveliness and grace prevail over adversity with well contoured, mutually enjoyed play (Katie's family would be an example). When a marked difference in parental styles or an infant's reluctance to engage made the goal of play difficult to achieve, the stressed alliance led to awkward communication, but the obstacles to organizing play would be overcome by the triad. With the triads who formed collusive alliances, conflicts between the parents led them to compete with each other for dominance and for the infant's attention. (Sonya's divorced parents in chapter 6 may be an example of placing unnegotiated parental conflict on the child.) Overt hostile interruption of the other or covert seductiveness by collusive parents led to a fragmented, frequently interrupted line of play (Mrs. S in chapter 7 was raised in this type of family system).

In the more seriously disrupted family system, attempts of the parents to elicit play and make transitions are confused. Approaches may be arbitrarily withdrawn or a participant excluded. Play is rigidified or disconnected. Affect is negative and no recovery of the goal of play occurs (Harry in chapter 5).

Observations of body, eye, and facial movements provide an insight into the process of communication within a triad. Effective transitions are brought about when readiness for a change of state is first preannounced nonverbally by a participant and then announced both nonverbally and verbally. The change is ratified by the others leading to a deconstruction of the state. The reconstruction that follows may leave a participant miscoordinated to the goals. Further reconstruction is required to repair the miscoordination and the formation of a new intact state.

The findings of this study of the triangular family system augments the extensive knowledge we have of dyadic communication. The study also moves from the attachment experimental design aimed at examining the dyad under conditions of danger and loss to understanding the triad as instituting moments of play. Correlations between attachment issues and triadic communication are speculative but inviting. Empathic sensitivity to others and to the self can be expected to facilitate both secure attachment in the dyad and cooperative alliance in the triad. Alternatively, communicative patterns of dismissive, avoidant, or anxious resistant preoccupation on the part of one or both parents increase the probability of a stressed or collusive alliance. Parental inclination, moreover, to moments of disorganization or dissociative dyadic communication under stress can be expected to contribute to unrepaired miscoordinations in a triadic goal.

The authors postulate that the patterns of nonverbal communication the infant forms in the triad will have a lasting effect. Whereas attachment research with over 25 years of well-documented findings demonstrates the probability of a lifelong effect on preverbal communicative patterns, triadic research as yet can demonstrate findings of continuity only for the first year. Nonetheless the family triangle study makes a promising beginning of opening family intercommunication to a well constructed research inquiry. Additionally, the categories of cooperative, stressed, collusive, and disorganized alliances strike a resonant note with clinical observations.

The Subjectivity Aware Sense of Self in an Intersubjective Matrix 9 to 15 Months

From day one, infants exist in an intersubjective matrix of dyads and triads influenced by and influencing the affective messages that pass back and forth within it. At about nine months, infants look to their caregivers' faces for explicit information about the caregivers' affective state and the guidance it provides. Affects again lead the way to the infant's double awareness. First, "I can be forewarned of danger or safety, of what to look at or what to avoid, when she is ready or when she is not." Second, "I can match my affect with hers, making me implicitly aware that I too have identifiable affects." Infants thereby take two big steps into the human world. First, guiding information is being communicated all the time through affect and this guidance can be sought. Second, a common bond, a form of fundamental twinship, exists in that all humans have similar feelings, and this commonality can be actively sought for confirmation or disconfirmation.

At the same time as affect checking begins, another change in information exchange is heralded by the pointing finger. For the younger infant, a parent's pointing finger is simply a passing source of interest to be looked at or grasped. Now the pointing finger becomes a directional signal for gaze focus. Older infants follow the finger, creating a line of gaze from their mother's eye to finger to an object or person at a distance. And infants use the same signal to alert others to their desire. In Stern's (1983) words, "Infants come upon the momentous realization that inner subjective experiences, the subject matter of the mind, are potentially shareable with someone else" (p. 128).

Seeking facial affective expressions and directional signals ushers in a new model of communication for infants. Previously, affect and gesture operated in a nonlinear fashion akin to the manner in which dance partners give bodily indications to each other of the flow of their movement. The coordination involves a trajectory. Stern has described the communication of affect to involve not only a recognition of the category (anger, joy, fear, etc.) but the rise or fall of affect insensity. Similarly, arousal is heightened (alertness) or lessened (boredom or drowsiness). These trajectories are what infant and mother learn to recognize in each other. Examples of this mode of communication in later life are a quarterback's "read" of a receiver's trajectory to connect on a pass or a boxer's counterpunch, which, to be effective, must anticipate the other boxer's blow before it begins as an actual movement. In the period in which the core sense of self develops, communication is asymmetrical. The infant's contribution is affect and gesture and in face-to-face communication, a coordination of timing of active facial expression and limb movements and pauses. The mother's contribution involves the use of three modes of communication: (1) the same coordinated timing of facial expression activity and pause; (2), the recognition of the baby's affect and gesture as signs signalling changes in state and motivational needs; and (3), the symbolic meaning of their immediate interplay stated in affective words and the deeper symbolism of their essential relational connection. The asymmetry can be stated in another way. Prior to 9 or 10 months infants begin to experience agency in communication as they activate expressions, vocalizings, and gestures. After 9 to 10 months the sense of agency is augmented by an increasing sense of intention as evidenced by intentional checking of mother's facial expression and the infant's pointing toward a desired object. Mother's agency and intentionality are integrated and organized through symbolic goals evidenced by the mother's inner monologue-dialogue, her spoken speech and her capacity for reflective awareness about her feelings and attitudes as they play out in her contacts and exchanges with her baby.

A fresh look at "stranger anxiety" (Spitz, 1965) through the lens of affective communication reveals an alternative explanation to that of the dawning capacity to differentiate the maternal representation. This previously offered explanation has been rendered unsatisfactory by evidence of the infant's discrimination of mother from strangers long before 10 months of age. At $9^{1}/_{2}$ months, Becca is taken to visit her grandmother. Her mother carefully introduces Becca to her new surroundings and, by the second day of the visit, the mother is out of the room when the grandmother enters with a stranger. Becca, who has just begun to stand, is noisily pulling herself up and down, using the sides of her crib. She interrupts her activity to glance first at her grandmother and then at the stranger. In a fast-paced sequence, her face goes from a flicker of a smile of greeting at her grandmother, to a look of apprehension as she glances past her grandmother at the stranger, to a look of fear and a decomposing of her fearful look into crying at a full glance at the stranger. Becca's mother, hearing her cry, calls to her from the hall. Becca stops crying and, by the time her mother approaches her, she is pulling up in a standing position with a beaming smile. Placed on her mother's lap, Becca ignores the stranger and plays a familiar game with her mother's earrings. She gives the stranger a few fleeting glances. Finally, her curiosity seems to win out over her apprehension; she reaches out to the stranger to inspect her necklace and then her face. Yet she positions her body so that she remains in or very near physical contact with her mother. As she moves toward the stranger, she glances back three different times, seemingly to inspect her mother's face. Her mother senses this as a request for reassurance and responds with encouragement.

Becca at 9 to 10 months reacts differently to the stranger than she would have earlier. At four months (Jaffe et al., 1999) conversational runs with a stranger add a mix of novelty, stress, and challenge comparable to the infant's being in a laboratory as compared to home. Especially for securely attached infants, this novelty triggers no fear. Even with less securely attached children, a stranger can elicit a conversational run but may have to work harder at it. Now at $9^{1}/_{2}$ months Becca, a securely attached child, decomposed rapidly from apprehension to fear and crying. The explanation that seems most plausible evolves from the new advance of looking to mother's familiar facial expression for an indication of safety or danger. This advance provides developing infants and toddlers an important orienting resource in navigating their way. What is newly strange about the "stranger" is that she is someone whose facial expression the infant cannot read. Extrapolated to culture, a source of the metaphor long used by Americans to refer to Asians as "inscrutable" lies in the formers' inability to use quickly an Asian's face for a safety providing orientation.

Returning to sign-signal communication, infants and toddlers look to their mother's face and body language to read a sign that signals both shared affect and orienting direction. Infants becoming excited look to mother to join in, whereas infants becoming frightened look to mother for confirmation of danger or reassurance of safety.

Not only the toddler's pointed finger but also vocalizing with grunts and, increasingly, words convey desire and its intensity. Agency and intention and increased mobility introduce to parents and toddler an inevitable series of conflicting agendas. To this often inflammatory mix is added what Spitz (1957) called the head-shaking NO! The gestural "no," with or without a vocalized word, communicates the toddler's emergent sense of the power of intention-driven opposition. Toddlers during this phase are not using "no" as a symbol stating in condensed form the sentence—"No, I do not want to play with this toy"—because they may then take the toy and play with it. They will say "No" not only to a food they don't prefer but to their favorite food as well. As toddlers suddenly discover they possess the power of a traffic red light or a stop sign, they want and need to practice its use to have available throughout life the capacity to signal refusal. A ubiquitous consequence is that parents and toddler are regularly immersed in communicative exchanges about signals of do and don't do, expressed through varying degrees of playfulness, conning, cooperating, and antagonistic opposition. As a background to these agenda struggles, parents are pulled between responding to the child's often confusing initiatives and attending to other concerns of their own.

Attachment at One Year and Its Intersubjective Communication

Findings derived from the Strange Situation Test and the Adult Attachment Interview (AAI) (Main, 2000) indicate the lived experiences of parent and child at one year. Based on subjecting toddlers to a controlled danger of a mother's departure from a play area and the presence of a stranger, four patterns of response have been categorized. Using an interview structured to focus on an adult's memory of his or her attachment experiences, four categories have been found that have a high probability of indicating what pattern of attachment the adult had formed at one year and the mode of attachment that the adult's offspring is likely to form with her or him.

Katie would fall into the category of 60% of toddlers who reveal patterns of secure attachment. They run to their parent, who responds to their distress and their appeal to be picked up, comforted, and then sensitively assisted to return to play with toys. Parents, such as Katie's, are identifiable by the AAI as "autonomous." By virtue of their own early secure attachment or later evolved capacity, "autonomous" adults confidently look to themselves for much of their security and to others when needed. As parents they demonstrate a capacity for reflective observation during their caregiving, play, spontaneous chatter, and informational exchanges.

To explicate the communicative aspect of the intersubjective world these parents and children co-create, we have attempted to put into words the communicative effect of the mixed linear and nonlinear nature of their exchanges. We see the message to be: "There is a you that I have come to know and there is a me you have come to know. We think well of each other. You have the space to be you with your needs and feelings, and I have the space to be me with my needs and feelings. I attend to you lovingly but neither dominate you nor let you dominate me. I try to attune my responses to your signs of hunger, thirst, being chilled or overheated, elimination, sleepiness, awakeness, playfulness, need for tactile and proprioceptive activity, hugging, and rocking. I try to sense when you are in distress and need me, or have had enough of me and want to be left alone to explore. Together you and I are establishing an intersubjective field in which my intuitive sense of you lets me track you and help you to track me. When I sense you are ready to take a step forward, I mirror it and share with you the joy of it and your appreciation (idealization) of me."

Ten percent of toddlers also run to their mothers. When picked up they push away rather than cling, and when put down they demand to be picked back up. These children have developed this unrewarding strategy in response to their parent's unpredictable oscillations between acceptance and angry rejection. In situations of danger or distress these toddlers combine anxious seeking with angry resistance. Parents whose own attachment was anxious-resistant will convey to their infant the carryover of their preoccupation with an unresolved struggle with their parents. In their care and chatter they communicate that at moments they can be sensitively concerned but that at other moments their feeling of fear, distress, anger, shame, or inadequacy will predominate. The message for the child is: "At times your mental state can be free to reflect your needs and feelings, but at especially critical times, my concerns about myself will lead me to fill your mind with my needs and troubled feelings." These children become unconsciously organized to be hypersensitive to their parent's aversive states. Many of these children, especially when their altruistic potential comes to the fore around the age of two (Zahn-Waxler and Radke-Yarrow, 1982), begin a lifelong pattern of preoccupied and often self-depleting caregiving to a parent and then others. The role reversal between child and parent may involve the parent's being dominated or infantilized. Other anxious-resistant children follow a pattern of seeking care but never getting enough. Their neediness frequently triggers aversive responses in others, leading the careseeker to affect states of shame, angry protest, and hurt withdrawal.

Twenty percent of toddlers do not approach their mothers on their return. Instead they seem to ignore both her departure and return. They focus on toys or actively move away. These children have experienced their mother as rejecting, threateningly intrusive, or, at the least, unavailable to satisfy the child's needs for security.

Parents who in their own attachments had an avoidant strategy to preserve what they could of contact with their caregiver will convey to their child that they have little intuitive potential for affective warmth and sensual closeness. In dialogue exchanges with their baby, avoidant parents are not apt to track in the midrange. In their broader response interactions, they may communicate an affectless devotion to duty and little sensitivity to distress and other messages the child sends. Kierra and her mother are examples. For the child the parent's message becomes: I recognize neither my nor your dependency needs. You had best empty your mind of recognition of your dependent wishes toward me. Furthermore, your protests about not having those needs and wishes responded to had best be suppressed too." These children, while appearing to be indifferent to their parent's activity, are actually experiencing considerable stress as evidenced by heightened cortisol levels. They become anxious hypervigilant observers calculating the range of physical and emotional closeness to, or distance from, their mothers that they need to maintain. Suppressing both their wishes for closeness and their hurt and anger at their rejection, their sense of self alone or with others becomes constricted and arid.

Ten percent of toddlers evince responses that signify the absence of a coherent strategy of behavioral or emotional organization (Hesse and Main, 2000). They may begin to move toward the returning mother appearing distressed, then stop, turn away, fall down, or freeze. They may go rapidly from distress to detachment with a trancelike facial expression. They may display odd stereotypic gestures. Many of these children have suffered direct abuse from their parents. Others have not been overtly maltreated but have been subjected to mothers who are frightened and/or frightening. For these children a move toward closeness arouses the fear of being frightened rather than comforted, while moving away means loss and abandonment at a moment of need. Action is paralyzed and the resulting affect state is chaotic. Their sense of self vacillates between high levels of anxiety and the dissociative cutting off of emotions.

Parents whose own childhood experiences left them vulnerable to disorganized affect states, disorientation at times of stress, and dissociative lapses will convey to their infants the fallout of their own chaotic sense of self. Their talk to their child will communicate the unpredictability of their concern; expressions of concern will alternate with sudden bursts of anger, abuse, or fright. The parent's unpredictable affective storms are made even more problematic for the child to orient to by the equally unpredictable lapses of the parent's attention into a state of detachment and dissociation. For the child, the parent's message becomes: "I cannot maintain my own self as consistently or purposefully organized. Whatever empathy I feel for myself or for you can be lost in a split second without any way for either of us to track the origins. I may be with you one minute, scaring you and myself the next, and off in a detached reverie the next." These children become hypervigilant to the world around them with fearful expectations. Their sense of self reflects many aspects of a chaotic fear that they will erupt and that others will erupt, or both, and that the boundaries between self and other will be obliterated. Signals of the danger of affective or aggressive eruption from self and/or other may trigger dissociation, while the absence of a relational connection may lead to a hunger for high-tension interactions of a provocative or sexual nature.

In instances of direct abuse or serious neglect, the message is: "You and your body are a dehumanized object to be subjected to unpredictable assault or abandonment." In the case of children being frightened by a caregiver who is angry or in states of panic or unreachable by virtue of being detached, drugged or dissociated, the message is: "Your emotional and bodily needs are insignificant in comparison to the distress dominating your mother's life." The child suffers the loss of a sense of coordination between body movement and intent, an asynchrony of the ordinary approach dance with mother at times of need. Play and the affect of playfulness (Meares, 1993; Lichtenberg and Meares, 1996) may be sacrificed. In addition, since the child can't establish a contingent relationship to the parent's unpredictable changes of affective-cognitive state, the child's long-term development of cognitive acuity and reflective capacity is often severely compromised (as with borderline patients).

HOW DO WE EXPLAIN THE DEVELOPMENT OF COMMUNICATION WITH SELF AND OTHER IN INFANCY? PART 2

Part 2: Modes of Symbolically Organized Experience and Communication (18 Months to Age 6 on)

The research on attachment categories indicates that well before the major transformation of symbolic organization that occurs at 18 months, highly organized patterns of communication between child and parents are firmly established, similarly or differently with each parent. Symbolic representation in the multiple modes of linear logical lexical processing (left hemisphere) and nonlinear sensory-metaphoric, imagistic processing (right hemisphere) moves the prior organization of relatedness and of communication into a dynamic flux. Older toddlers now live in complexly organized, different modes of experience. The multiple modes of verbal and nonverbal processing create so great a change in the developing child's experience that both Edelman and Damasio describe it as the advent of a higher or extended form of consciousness. The altered experience creates new possibilities of communication with others and with self.

Rather than positing a dichotomy between linear and nonlinear modes of cognition, Hartmann (1999) describes a continuum of processing ranging across focused waking thought, looser, less structured waking thought, reverie and daydreaming to dreaming. Focused waking thought allows for communication in logical sequences using words, numbers, and culturally agreed on arbitrary signs. Specificity of meaning is adhered to and monitoring through self-reflection and anticipation of reception by the audience sets boundaries of tact and plausibility. Less structured waking thought is more compatible with communication in play and action. In this less linear mode, sticks become spoons for feeding dolls who become one's self. Folded paper becomes airplanes that can take one to the stars. Metaphor, puns, nonsense, rhyming make communication more spontaneous, less monitored and less subject to self-reflection. Alternatively, reverie and daydreaming are primarily modes of inner communication, whose time of origin in childhood is difficult to ascertain. While REM sleep exists at birth and dreams have been described by two-year-olds (Freud, 1900, pp. 130–131), the inner communicative significance of the remembered dream varies with age and person. Dreams retain characteristics of core consciousness in that they are totally present-centered and devoid of self-reflection. They resemble nonlinear waking thought in their imagery, use of pictorial metaphor, and loosening of categorical boundaries so that associative connections are more easily made. Dreams also retain another essential feature of core consciousness in that they are "guided by the emotions and the emotional concerns of the dreamer" (Hartmann, 1999, p. 785). But dreaming also differs from emergent core consciousness. Whereas emergent core consciousness places emotion in the context of an ongoing here-and-now sense of self-interacting with the world around, dreaming provides an imagistic context for emotion. Along with the relatively definable modes of awake and sleep experience, a less formulated continuous flow of self-state information derives from body movements, gurgles, and other sounds of tension and relaxation, in changes in breathing, vocal tone, pauses, ums and ers, and flickers of facial expression. These are constituent communicative aspects from and to the self and others that lie at the edge of core consciousness but are generally too ephemeral for reflection or symbolization.

After the middle of the second year, communication between parent and child combines a mixture of words and actions.

Sometimes the words (as symbolic communication) prevail, but for long periods actions on both sides dominate communication. The entry of toddlers into the symbolic world changes the dynamic of their relationship to their parents and to themselves. Children's comprehension of language, of spoken commands and references, heightens parents' expectations of them. There follows inevitable tension that culminates in what Mahler (1968) referred to as a rapprochement crisis. In contrast, the explanation we offer is that with greater symbolic capacity comes greater independence of agendas on the part of the older toddler. This is met by greater expectations by parents that parental rules and restrictions can be understood and responded to. In many small moments of daily life this expectation is confirmed. However, when agendas are more strongly in opposition, parental patience is strained, with aversive affects coming to the fore. The paradoxical effect is that the toddler's recently acquired symbolic capacity for word understanding and exchanges is lost and a regressive resort to distress, confusion, and obstinance often ensues. Alternatively, older toddlers entry into the symbolic world provides the opportunity for the playing out of scenarios that allow them to be more personally self-expressive, work out the puzzles of experience that constantly arise, and learn more about themselves. The experience of toddlers with a mirror exemplifies these developments.

A mirror elicits a response of delight in infants between nine and 12 months of age. They will laugh, coo, and jiggle their bodies with excitement. At this age, if the mirror is distorted, they show no change in reaction, and if a label or smudge is placed on their foreheads or nose, they display no notice of it. Each movement the infant makes instantly influences the percept. The mirror has the same property to entertain as a mobile or an animated cartoon, but with the infant as creative director. In one experiment, infants viewed themselves through a videotape monitor. As soon as the picture frame of the monitor was frozen, the infants stopped being delighted and highly active (T. Modarressi, personal communication).

Infants between 13 and 15 months react differently to the mirror. When confronted with their mirror images, these toddlers grow sober, pensive, and less active. If the mirror is distorted, they focus on it intently, without pleasure. They will notice a label surreptitiously placed on their foreheads or a smudge on their nose, and may even reach for it in the mirror, but they do not touch it on their own face.

Between 15 and 21 months a dramatic change occurs. Toddlers who have surreptitiously had a smudge placed on the nose (Brooks and Lewis, 1976; Lewis and Brooks-Gunn, 1979) or a label on the forehead (Modarressi and Kenny, 1977; Modarressi, 1980) will, when exposed to a mirror, reach up and touch their noses or foreheads. Amsterdam and Levitt (1980) find this reaction more reliably between 18 and 22 months. What this suggests is that at this age children have discovered that the mirror will not only "capture" and reflect visual information about an image but will also convey information about themselves.

The toddler's recognition that the mirror conveys information about the self adds a new discovery. To put the experience in words (which of course the child could not use), the toddler discovers: "That object out there—the mirror—contains an image that is unlike all other images in that it stands for me. Moreover, the image of me has been changed—I don't usually have a label on my forehead or a smudge on my nose." The object (the mirror) is both concrete—it exists on its own—and abstract—it can mirror something else. The image in the mirror also has concrete properties—it exists and conveys information ("It tells me how I look, that a label is on my forehead or a smudge is on my nose that I didn't know was there"). More abstractly, the viewer (the "I" implicitly, not reflectively) exists as an image with a known, expectable appearance. ("I can see my image, just as I see those of others around me.")

Children after two respond quite differently (Modarressi, 1981). These children will remove the label, examine it, and even use the mirror to replace it on their foreheads. The awareness that the mirror image is theirs becomes consciously reflected on recognition, usually accompanied by a smile. At times, the children have a sense of surprise, even awe. If the mirror surface is altered to produce a distorted image, these older children will react with a dramatic change from pleasurable interest to acute alarm and distrust. It is as though the concrete, distinct image of self they worked so hard to consolidate conceptually had dissolved before their eyes.

The mirror observations point to toddlers growing awareness of themselves as an entity. "Self" the word thereby becomes a symbol for self, the entity, a person named Tom or Carol. And Tom can converse with Tom just as mother converses with him and he with her, although the conversation with himself will differ increasingly from spoken speech (Vygotsky, 1962).

As memories of events that had occurred in the presymbolic period are experienced as integrally congruent with the symbolizing child's sense of self, earlier maps become recategorized and remapped in symbolic form. At 13 months during the period of sign-signal communication, Liz began to object vigorously to her eight-year-old sister's sitting on their mother's lap. Liz would grunt, push her sister off, or, if that failed, raise such a fuss that mother and sister would good-naturedly comply. Liz and her sister had a generally excellent relationship, and her sister willingly shared in her caretaking. At 13 months Liz was communicating using an emphatic gestural signal to express her possessiveness and territoriality. After 18 months, Liz began to give increasingly symbolic verbal and play-action versions to a concept of "mine," my mother, and my space. At two years, she would run to her father for roughhouse play, but when her father embraced her mother, she vehemently protested: "No, you have your own Mommy!"

Language and Play

Language, Bruner (1983) states, "begins when mother and infant create a predictable format of interaction that can serve as a microcosm for communicating and for constituting a shared reality" (p. 18). The remarkable acquisition of vocabulary and grammatical construction that occurs from 18 to 36 months can easily obscure the amount and type of preparation that exists before the subsequent upsurge of verbal communication. Infants are bathed in the "chatter" of their tending caregiver accompanied by exaggerated orofacial and gestural displays. Kaye (1982) recorded 13,574 utterances from 36 mothers of young babies. The mother's conversation depended on pretending (playing) that a dialogue was going on. Mothers who talk to their babies invoke a panoply of descriptions of their mutual activities, value statements, markers of recognition of states, as well as illustrating the formal elements of discourse. "All right, sweetheart, I hear you. You're telling me you're hungry. OK, I'm coming." Or "Oh, no. You scratched me. That's not a good little boy. Well I guess I'll have to cut your nails again." Talk swirls all around the infant and young toddler. Talk directed to the child, talk about the child, talk between the parents in the child's hearing—all create an affective ambiance that tilts either toward dynamic representational schemas or toward working models of secure or insecure attachment.

Language usage and form as indicated by the Adult Attachment Interview and by the capacity or limitation to free associate is influenced strongly by the presence or absence of playfulness in the pretend dialogue of mother and baby. A remarkable example of the acquisition of language under conditions of play is demonstrated by the accidental acquisition of learned use of language by a bonobo monkey named Kanzi (Savage-Rumbaugh et al., 1993). A team of researchers attempted to teach Mateta, a bonobo ape caught in the wild, to master a representational use of symbols. The effort, carried out over four years, was a failure. Kanzi, her baby, was present during this time. Serendipitously the researchers discovered that Kanzi not only learned the geometric symbols, but also demonstrated an understanding of spoken language.

Kanzi was never rewarded and no effort was made to teach him; he was simply in the area playing. The researchers note that Kanzi, exactly like the human infant, was exposed to spoken language in a natural pragmatic surrounding. He developed comprehension because he had the innate brain capacity to organize sound and gesture into language that he could use to predict events in his environment. The researchers set up two model playhouses in which instructions were given without the speaker being seen to rule out gestural guides. Kanzi was tested in one playhouse and Alia, the two-and-a-half-year-old daughter of one of the researchers, in the other. For both Kanzi and Alia the researchers found it necessary to maintain an atmosphere of playfulness by making a game of the testing. If the atmosphere turned serious both would balk. As relatively equal comprehenders of spoken language, both Kanzi and Alia easily carried out such instructions as "Go get the carrot that's in the microwave" and many more complex action assignments. But the symbolic capacity of Kanzi went beyond this type of compliance. When told to wet the (toy) snake, Kanzi did not take the snake to the wash basin as the researchers expected but opened the door and threw it out in the rain! Moreover, given the instruction "feed your ball some tomato," Kanzi picked up a toy tomato and briefly put it down while he looked around for a ball. He chose a soft sponge ball with a pumpkin face that he put into his lap and then placed the tomato into the mouth on the face embedded in the ball. The authors concluded that both child and bonobo understood that toys were pretend (a toy snake) and not real animals. Bonobos clearly possess the early stages of symbolic play—certainly equal to a two-and-a-half-year-old child and maybe a three- or four-year-old, but that would seem at this time to be as far as their brain's resourcefulness will stretch.

The research on Kanzi's serendipitous acquisition of a working knowledge of English points to the necessity to distinguish between language comprehension and linguistic expression. The bonobo infant's brain is constituted so that when exposed to the same conversational interactions that occur during the daily life of human infants, the neural networks form in support of linguistic comprehension. But these brain networks that support comprehension are but one component of the total network systems that make possible the full range of human symbolic usage. In the human, comprehension precedes expression, and expression in the form of speech is made possible by a vocal apparatus capable of forming consonants as well as vowels. The human is thus capable of practicing the use of language both in listening and, unlike other primates, in speaking. The result is a further differention of self—to be a listener to others and to speak to others in a manner that conveys one's wishes and meanings, and to speak to and listen to oneself. Kanzi's accomplishment with comprehension notwithstanding, we do not imagine he ever developed much of an inner dialogue replete with reviews of the day's events and his feelings about them, complete with playful rememberings and revisions. The difference between the bonobo and the developing child does not have to do with symbol usage per se, of which both are capable; rather it concerns the type of symbol usage available to each. The bonobo is limited to rudimentary (two- to three-year-old human) language grammar and symbolic imagination. The differences are believed to be due to the properties of neural systems that indirectly support language learning and language use in human beings. We can no longer consider specialized brain areas as specific to language or speech. In language learning at any moment, the contribution of brain regions that specialize in the extraction of sensory detail may be proportionally different from regions that analyze the integration of information across auditory, visual, tactile, olfactory, and gustatory modalities. In language usage, symbolic representational memory, and symbolic play, the whole brain participates using networks that combine maps of specific functions with numerous reentrant associational pathways.

The transformational impact of language and nonlinguistic symbolization is so profound that Damasio and Edelman both regard it as the foundation of a higher, more extended mode of consciousness. In Edelman's term, the brain "boot straps" itself into a different mode of mapping and categorization by recategorizing, remapping, and adding reentrant communicative signals. In this process many previous maps of presymbolic lived experience are recreated that provide continuity between preverbal and verbal experiences, especially the rich affective experience of early life. With symbolization, the range of cognitive capacity greatly expands. For example, children can successively touch all of the objects in one category followed by successive touching of objects in a different category. They can plan more complex block construction and are more apt to use conventional scripts in play with toys, dolls, and soldiers. All of this coordinates with the use of language to express agreement with, or opposition to, the agendas of others. As the brain's resources of perceptual recognition, conceptual categorization, and affective discrimination increase, the potentiality for symbolic usage to map actual experience and imagine alternative scenarios also increases. Consciousness expands to increased observation of the self interacting with people and inanimate objects. Language permits children to form a monologue with themselves and a dialogue with others, real and imagined, in which the realm of observation becomes registered (Vygotsky, 1962).

Three Realms of Lived Experience

The lived experience of a child of two, three, and four years flows back and forth among three realms: (1) a realm of learning to recognize, communicate, and work out ways to deal with the exigencies of daily life, characterized by serious earnest effort; (2) a realm of symbolic play alone or with others, with toys and words, characterized by an affect of playfulness and an exploratory imagination; and (3) a realm of personal registry of impressions expressed in inner conversation that is often unself-consciously spoken aloud.

Whether serious and earnest or playful and imaginative, lived experiences are organized as events that become little stories or dramas with a beginning, middle, and end. The studies of event knowledge reported by Nelson (1986) provide a basis that is essential to our understanding. She notes that "phenomenologically the world is experienced as a series of ongoing events" (p. 4) and that "children as young as 3 years are sensitive to the temporal structure of events and are able to report action sequences of familiar events virtually without error" (p. 231). Children of three years can easily be tested about their experiencing of events, but, more difficult to confirm, evidence supports a conclusion that event representation occurs as early as one year. Moreover, as we can expect from the pragmatic requirements of information mapping, young children form generalized expandable schemas of the events they experience. Asked to tell about making cookies, a child of three responds, "Well, you bake them and eat them," and a child of four years, five months answers, "My mommy puts chocolate chips inside the cookies. Then ya put 'em in the oven. . . . Then we take them out, put them on the table and eat them" (p. 27). These examples demonstrate the use of the timeless verb and the general "you" form and the accuracy of sequence. Older children progressively produce longer, more detailed accounts, but the essential form and content are identical. "The generalization of an experience appears to be a natural product of the child's mind. . . . As more episodes of the same type are experienced, memories of them become more skeletal and general" (p. 232).

The essential organization of the generalized event mapping is temporal and causal. In a restaurant event, "the action of entering the restaurant results in the new state of being inside. Being inside, in turn, enables you to go to your table. The succession of causal and enabling connections is what moves you through the actions of the event" (p. 51). Nelson (1986) notes the provocative finding that, in describing their event knowledge:

> Young children use relational constructions and linguistic terms that reveal an understanding of logical relationships in advance of that usually attributed to them. Hypothetical and conditional relations are appropriately noted by forms such as "if . . . then" or "when x then y." Causal relations are expressed by "because" and "so." Temporal relations are expressed by "then" but also by "before," "after," and "first." . . . Adversative relations are coded by "but," and alternatives by "or" [pp. 232–233].

Unlike older children and adults, young children's accounts of events do not include settings, sources, or emotions such as likes and dislikes. In their earnest efforts to tell a story, answer a question, and work out problems, young children are often extremely vulnerable to being shamed, teased, and ridiculed. Frequently their mode of communicating their aversive response to such wounds to self-esteem is via temper outbursts.

Stern (1985, 1990) distinguishes between discourse organized in the form of an internal monologue of an experience world and discourse organized in the form of a spoken narrative of a story world. Both contain the theme or context of life events selected from the totality of daily exposure. In the experience world, the child constantly constructs what to attend to, what current themes to elaborate, and what new ones to design. Stern (1990) gives the example of Joey at four years using both types of discourse to elaborate an aggression theme from a day's experience of hitting a girl. "Joey relives the scene of hitting the girl and feeling himself seen by other people as dangerous and bad. He reexperiences his feelings of alienation, shame, his being put in his room, his making noise and loud music to express his anger to comfort himself" (p. 148). In his experience world, Joey makes frequent references to his feelings. In contrast, in the story he tells of the same event, references to feelings are relatively few. The same event organization constructed in the experience world is now reconstructed into a story to be presented to an audience. He renders the story in the form of an action sequence. "I played," " He hides." He streamlines the events and makes the rendering more dramatic by a small change in the sequence. He also uses disguises, lion for himself as hitter to reduce his embarrassment and potential censure. In contrast to an absence of emotions in a child's description of events to a questioner, affects and sensations are richly represented in the child's internal lived experience and monologue about it.

In the realm of learning to recognize, deal with, and converse about exigencies, children employ principally linear reasoning in conjunction with parental guides and prohibitions. Significant learning about the rules of interactions also comes from peer play (Damon, 1988). Rather than peer play's being based on parental authority alone, the need to take turns and accept the claims of others can be appreciated directly from consequences to the self of unregulated acts of aggressive antagonistic behavior.

Along with procedural memory, event memory helps the child to organize lived experiences into categories such as getting dressed, eating, going to school or the store, or zoo, or to visit grandma. The upsurge of acquisition of language fills out the slots in event memory, building more complex communications out of the basic structure of a linear organized sentence. Older toddlers are skilled at distinguishing pretend play from "reality." They use this distinction constantly to cope with the emotional impact of conflictual situations. However, before the age of four or five they have little ability to question the validity of a perception or a belief. Thus, for the early sense of self, a perception carries with it the sense of a veridical belief, and a belief carries the conviction of there being no alternatives. Thus a conviction of truth as the child views it will be stated as an absolute often leading to clashes with older children and parents.

Beginning with syntactic and imagistic symbolization, inferences about the self with other are created (Weiss and Sampson, 1986). The content of these inferences lead to patterns of conceptual organization that underly identity and relational expectations. An inference may or may not be expressed in explicit communication to the self or to others; rather it may be elaborated in unconscious fantasy dreams, or concretized in symptoms. A patient inferred the belief that she was and is a freak because her large body at birth led her weight-preoccupied mother to place her on a diet of skim milk at 10 days. An avoidantly attached child may infer he is evil and had better stay away from his mother because he causes her distress. Alternatively he may infer he must keep his distance because she is a witch who causes him harm. An ambivalent-anxiously attached child may infer she must remain closely preoccupied with her mother because her mother needs her. She may regard herself as an all-powerful rescuer. Another child may stay near her mother or any substitute she can find, because she sees herself as weak, ineffectual, and dependent. Inferences such as evil child and witch mother exist psychically not as separate entities but coexist with one dominant, the other latent. Dualistic maps of self derive from the finding that interactional attachment patterns "are a mutually organized and mutually understood code in which any role implies its reciprocal, neither can be represented without the other" (Beebe, Lachmann, and Jaffe, 1997, p. 173). Thus role responses of caregiver and careseeker, of victimizer-victim, of intrusive-avoidant will typi-cally coexist in the sense of self. The dominant belief of the patient who regarded herself as an overweight freak coexisted with a belief she was irresistably attractive to men. When the freak self-image was guiding her expectations she became reclusive and suicidal. When the attractive view guided her expectations, she was ebul-lient, charming, and flirtatious.

An Autobiographic Self: The Created Story of Personal Identity

Children of four to six years continuously form two stories they tell to themselves and others. One story creates the sense of who they are, an autobiographic self. The other story creates a plan for the future, an illusory-to-become self such as found in the oedipal fantasy.

Damasio observes that "autobiography memory is architec-turally connected, neurally and cognitively speaking, to the non-conscious protoself and to the emergent and conscious core self of each lived instant. This connection forms a bridge between the ongoing (transient) process of core consciousness . . . and a pro-gressively larger array of established rock-solid memories per-taining to unique historical facts and consistent characteristics of an individual . . . for instance, where you were born, and to whom: critical events in your autobiography; what you like and dislike; your name; and so on. Although the basis for the autobiograph-ical self is stable and invariant, its scope changes continuously as a result of experience" (1999, p. 173). Damasio notes that the autobiographic self image constitutes a healthy background, "often just hinted and half guessed . . . ready to be made central if the need arises to confirm that we are who we are" (p.174).

Damasio's view of the autobiographic self connects immedi-ate core consciousness with the forms of memory that are explicit—episodic memory and semantic memory. The sense of a biographic self that arises from this bridging permits a child to say to herself and others "My name is Helen. I live in the yellow house on the corner. I have a doll house my daddy made for me and I play with my sister and my friend Jane." However, Damasio's focus on the "rock-solid" memories of pertinent facts accounts for only a small segment of the autobiographic story of self we tell to others and to ourselves. For example, we may tell to others explicitly and to ourselves implicitly who we believe ourselves to be through our posture, our gait, our verbal tone, our greeting smile, the frown marks on our forehead. All these manifestations of our sense of self may be conscious or unconscious. They may draw on non-conscious procedural memory or on current intention. They may be ingrained and persistent or ephemeral, depending on the context of the moment. We would argue that only in a limited way can we regard our experience of our sense of self as resting on a bedrock of immutable facts. Rather we tell ourselves and others a shifting panoply of stories depending on our dominant motivation and the intersubjective context as it bears on that motivation. The body sense of self carries into our biographic story a history of past physiological regulation or dysregulation. The sense of self in an intimate relationship brings with it one or more attachment categories, the memory of which is recreated with a particular current person. The story of our prior interests, the intensity with which we explore them, the kind of preferences for play, imagination, and contemplation we lean toward, are influential in our messages to ourself and others, especially during childhood with peers, playmates and teachers. The sense of self when responding aversively to internal or external stimuli involves patterns of doing, relating, and being that affect large areas of who we are. What is the "story of me" at times of crisis, in the midst of controversy, during danger? Am I resilient or vulnerable to shame and embarrassment, to loss, to success or failure? How do I juggle the pain of truth, the ease to practice deception? Finally, can I enjoy sensuality or am I left with what seems like an insatiable desire for either soothing or stimulating touch, or am I fearful and avoidant of intimate contact? In my sense of self can sexual excitement be integrated with relational attachment or has it become dissociated, creating a state of troubled excitation?

A principal contribution to who we tell ourselves and others that we are lies in Freud's discovery of the dynamic unconscious and the oedipal-Electra myths. As Damasio points out, the four-to six-year-old child has some rock-solid facts to draw on to stabilize an autobiographic story. But as Freud discovered, the child of the same age has a world of conscious and unconscious beliefs, fantasies, and dreams. This realm of nonlinear experience creates a dynamic flux between the possibility and probability of who we tell ourselves we are, were, and will become. At any moment the child's biographic story demands negotiation between the more fixedly known and the more loosely chimeric. The biographic story that will emerge at any moment from this negotiation will be heavily influenced by the audience to whom it is directed. All stories have their edges, their selecting of what to include, what to exclude, and what deception to aim for. The Rashomon effect arises not only from multiple observers; each child is his or her own Rashomon depending on need, desire, and audience. Sandy, a four-and-a-half-year-old, overheard his mother pleading with his reluctant father to buy her a new car. Sandy appeared with his coin bank and announced that he would take his mother to buy her the car. As the astonished parents paused in their argument, Sandy had a new thought. He added, "but mother you'll have to hold my hand as we cross the street." In this story, two strands of Sandy's biographic message of who he is converge. First, he is the confident loving and loved son-rescuer-husband-to-be of his mother. Their past—the love between them, their present—her need for rescue and his resources, their future all coalesce in a burst of pride as to who he is and what he can do: he will be an improved version of his father. This is one Rashomon view of the situation. In a second version, Sandy sees himself in the restricted capacities of his four-and-a-half years as he pictures himself in the outer world of dangers not yet mastered. This version is closer to the bedrock of personal fact in two ways: Sandy is still a little boy and a parent's hand is the sustaining resource for his courage and confidence. And yet another version of Sandy's identity is based on the power of body-based metaphor to symbolize moments of tension in close family attachments. Here the courage to step between father and mother, to push father aside, and take possessive hold of mother would be symbolically analogous to the penetration into space of both the whole body and the erect penis. But a street (open space) contains its own dangers as symbolized by cars and reinforced by the inevitable sight of smashed animals easily analogous to the overwhelming hurting power of an irate father-rival. This is a version more likely to be told to the self and others in symbolic play, drawings, and dreams. The final contribution to Sandy's biographic self draws on Kohut's concept of a normal oedipal phase. In this view, Sandy would draw on his memory of his closeness with his basically protective father not to see him as a threatening ogre frightening Sandy into passivity or panic. He would recognize that his mother does not put him into the position of expecting him to be her sexual partner and exposing him to the incredible deflation of his bodily limitations. And he would have a view of himself as seen through both parents' eyes that mother is proud of his love and devotion to her just as his father is proud of his enthusiasm and enterprise.

Freud's discovery of the triangular fantasies of the oedipal phase led to the conviction that these conscious and then repressed schemas provided a psychoanalytic bedrock to each individual's unconscious biographic self. The initial certainty of the centrality of each child's oedipal (Electra) myth to identity and potential pathology has eroded over time. Claims made by separation- individuation, attachment, Kleinian, and other theorists emphasize the significance of preoedipal experiences. Observers of later periods such as adolescence, the period of transition to adult life, the midlife period, and even the later life stage point to the contribution of postoedipal experiences to alter the coloration and even some basic aspects of who we are to ourselves and others. Trauma at any stage of life has the power to affect our sense of self, to shatter our self-confidence, and to freeze us in a time frame of reliving the sense of self as victim or turn us to hatred and vengeance. Very early trauma, such as that of the infant who drew the inference that she was a monstrous freak, can affect the sense of self at each stage of development. Inner voices of a negative sense of self can become cripplingly (suicidally) manifest at any unpredictable moment. Traumatizing events such as the Holocaust, war, imprisonment, shootings, and vehicular catastrophes can disrupt and shatter, often permanently, an existing sense of self.

From the vantage point of a contemporary concept of a biographic sense of self, what remains of the salience of the oedipal phase? We suggest a major contribution to development lies in the establishment of a time line to our sense of self. From this period on, we live our experiences more or less "realistically" as they unfold (the now or core consciousness), but guided by an illusion of a future. The triangular fantasy provides the power or impetus for the story of an identity plan the child creates that he or she organizes along the plot line of "when I grow up." The compelling nature of the drama of the projected oedipal plan lies in the child's being able to integrate stories of attachment, rivalry, gender, and body and relational exploration. Variants are built out of components of the integrated romantic story, such as the career (lawyer, doctor, astronaut) to be pursued "when I grow up." We describe the mind play on the time line of the future that begins with the oedipal phase and continues throughout life as illusions. The illusions of the future range from daydreams, fanciful or realizable, to relatively concrete planning, and they range from private to shared. We distinguish illusions on the time line from pretend play. Pretend play begins prior to a well defined time line. During pretend play the child maintains a firm distinction between make believe and real, between the doll and the real mother, the play teddy bear and a live animal. With illusion, the distinction between what is hoped for and what is realizable is often indistinct, allowing hope to persist under adverse conditions. Similarly the distinction between what is dreaded and what is likely to be actualized may remain fuzzy, leading to wariness, suspicion, and pessimism as integral to both a present and future sense of self.

Of course, illusions about who we are, were, and will be are constantly being renegotiated. A primary mode of the renegotiation takes place in inner speech and self-reflection integrated with shifts in the intersubjective flow of daily life. Sometimes a dramatic effort is made to rewrite the past as in the family romance of a royal birth. Authors such as William Faulkner and Patrick

O'Brien have invented different pasts, even different names for themselves. In conclusion, we suggest that a paradox exists between a universal notion that a cohesive sense of self includes the solidity of a biographic identity, and the persistent flux of the story we tell to ourselves and others about who we are, were, and especially will become. Too loose a story leaves us aimless and disoriented, easily subject to dissociation. Too fixed a story leaves us inflexibly unable to navigate through the inevitable transitions. And from the clinical side, the story of the biographic self as told to the self in inner monologue-dialogue and to the analyst and reflected back empathically by the analyst must be open to reformulation for a therapeutic effect to result.

CHAPTER THREE

OPEN FLEXIBLE COMMUNICATION IN MOMENT-TO-MOMENT EXCHANGES

In this chapter and the four to follow we describe our approach to clinical work. Throughout these chapters we illustrate our proposal that a spirit of inquiry in the form of exploration or inquisitiveness is an ever-present dimension of communication in psychoanalytic therapy. In chapters 1 and 2 we illustrated that development can be charted as a process of ever-increasing complexity of communication, privately with oneself and between oneself and with others. Abstractions, metaphors, symbols and signs, in fact, all forms of affective information are packaged in this monologue-dialogue that underlies all communicative techniques. In this chapter we sketch the seesaw path of communication in analytic history and present a clinical vignette that describes the nuanced view of an open flexible communication, which we espouse.

In the evolution of psychoanalytic technique, the process of communication originated with a conversational dialogue. Freud made his initial, seminal formulations by "talking" with his patients. A clear illustration is found in his discussion of Katharina, Case 4 in the "Studies on Hysteria" (Breuer and Freud, 1893). Katharina approached Freud as he was resting after his climb up a mountain and asked him about her symptoms. Freud recognized their hysterical origin and wondered privately, "was I to make an attempt at an analysis? I could not venture to transplant hypnosis to these altitudes, but perhaps I might succeed with a simple talk. I should have to try lucky guesses" (p. 127). And so he did. As Katharina struggled to recall the sexual scenes and experiences that were associated with her hysterical anxiety attacks, Freud suggested to her, "if you could remember now what was happening in you at the time, when you had your first attack, what you thought about it—it would help you" (p. 128). At that time, private monologues-dialogues, inquiry and simple talk, provided the foundation for the technique that was to supplant hypnosis.

Quite rapidly, after Freud's "simple talk," psychoanalytic technique evolved in an opposite direction, helped along this route by Freud's technique papers and Glover's (1955) systematization of psychoanalytic techniques. As Lichtenberg (1994) has pointed out, in his technique papers, Freud, frightened by incidents of immorality around him, primarily admonished analysts what not to do. By implication, avoiding the "don'ts" became a model for good technique as though an analysis would follow a natural course toward the resolution of conflicts so long as the analyst did not gratify or contaminate the transference and fixate the libido onto his person. Based on the libido theory as a model, suggesting or advising (for example, Freud's own suggestion to Katharina "if you could remember . . . it would help") or ordinary talk, might entail libidinal gratifications for the patient. Gratification once unleashed on some occasions could open the door to some compromising behavior on the part of the analyst. Communicative restraint, parsimonious and precise interpretations of the transference manifestations, became the prescribed regimen for analysts. Not to talk and not to reveal became values analysts-in-training had to learn. Patients had to adapt to the silences and repetitive patterns of behavior of analysts as modes of communication while analysts tilted away from their need to adapt to the patient's mode.

What began as a spirit of inquiry became a rigorous effort by analysts to speak only when interpreting the patient's associations. Furthermore, interpretations were often only given when the associations revealed primarily oedipal transferences. What began as Freud's lucky guesses became "unlucky" for those analysands whose analysts considered their interpretations not as "guesses" but as "rock-bottom" truths. In turn, these "truths" were derived from two sources: a model of early development based on reconstructions from the analyses of adults; and a model of the mind based on Freud's structural theory (Lachmann and Beebe, 1992).

The privileging of silence and abstinence as techniques was based on the premise that the analyst-patient dialogue should originate solely from the patient's communications. These communications were viewed either as associations or as resistances to associations to the analyst's interpretations. In the analytic dialogue, the flexible, conversational, "lucky guess" aspects of communication was supplanted by a more rigidly defined interpretive mode that was inextricably tied to the libidinal drive-discharge theory. In this mode of communication, silence came to mean the analyst was waiting for the patient to say the "right" thing for an oedipal (or preoedipal) conflict interpretation.

These presumptions confined the analyst primarily to the role of a responder to the associations and dreams of the patient. But, more to the point, such a bias underestimates the quality and potential variety of the analyst's participation. It is this participation that we describe as the internal monologue and dialogue that is part and parcel of the analytic encounter. The analyst's bias would inevitably combine many sources and personal meanings. For example, vivid private associations may prompt especially close listening, or, a patient's associations may fail to meet the expectations of the analyst. Then the analyst might feel bored, drowsy, and irritated at having to listen again to such "pseudo-associations." The analyst may even feel deeply moved and in private reveries in which he or she moves associatively in and out of the patient's life. These communicative connections of the analyst may or may not be revealed to the patient. In that instance the patient may turn to the analyst to try to sense his or her impact on the analyst's state of mind. In recognition of the complexity of the interaction, both in theory and in practice, contemporary analysts have sought to reconceptualize the ways in which they communicate with their patients.

As different theories evolved, a tower of babel fell on both free association and interpretation. Different psychoanalytic theories organize the patient's associations differently. Hearing their patients differently, practitioners of these different approaches then come up with a wide range of interventions. One overarching assumption has, until recently, however, remained unchallenged: communication means talking, and other forms of communication, bodily posture, somatic symptoms, and varieties of "acting out" or "enactments," constituted either resistances to, or pathologies of, free association. Such mavericks needed to be corralled. The analyst needed to bring them into conformity with the expectation that communication referred to a verbal modality. Only then could the "nonverbal" communications be analyzed and interpreted. This formulation is a remnant of the time prior to the recognition of procedural learning as an equal partner with symbolized or episodic memories in the communication between any partners, whether mother and infant or analyst and patient (Lyons-Ruth, 1999; Lichtenberg, 1989; Lichtenberg, Lachmann, and Fosshage, 1996; Stern et al., 1998).

Analysts have long recognized that in the treatment of children, play and nonverbal communication in the form of play (including their own self-involvement) provides the communications required to understand the child's struggles. Yet even here, the aim has frequently been to translate the knowledge gained from the play with dolls, soldiers, or other fantasy games of traumatic experiences, into verbal interpretations of the unconscious wishes and fears that were talked about outside the pretend world. Without a verbal statement, child analysts feared the playing out of inner turmoil would have little or no effect. Furthermore, the recognition of an extensive idiosyncratic, nonverbal language that was discovered in work with psychotic patients required a reassessment of the limits of verbal discourse as the only relevant mode of analytic communication (Sullivan, 1962; Atwood, 2001).

Of the founders of psychoanalysis, no one was more concerned about its communicative aspects than Ferenczi. His paper "Confusion of Tongues" (1933), on the misunderstandings between children and adults and between analysts and analysands with respect to "intentions," stands as an example of the spirit of communication to which we subscribe. Using parents' denial of sexual abuse as a basis, Ferenczi made the telling point that a trauma, however bad, is made far worse by "gaslighting," that is, corrupting the child's sense of reality, as for example when the adult pretends that a trauma event never occurred. In this circumstance, the child may have to forfeit his or her own sense of reality to maintain the attachment to the adult.

In the dialectic between the value of an analyst's nonrevelation to avoid muddying the waters of the transference and the analyst's self-disclosures, including the acknowledgment of feelings, values, attitudes, actions, and intentions, Ferenczi often weighed heavily on the side of disclosure. Published in 1933, his paper illustrates the direction in which Ferenczi was moving: recognition of bidirectional influence of the analyst-patient relationship. The paper is remarkable in that Ferenczi reconceptualized resistance and the then generally accepted notion that patients resisted getting better because they derived gratification from their adherence to their pathology. Ferenczi wrote, "As the state of the patient, even after a considerable time, did not change in essentials, I had to give free rein to self criticism. I started to listen to my patients when, in their attacks, they called me insensitive, cold, even hard and cruel . . . I began to test my conscience in order to discover whether . . . there might be some truth to these accusations" (p. 157).

Ferenczi's work contrasts his own pioneering efforts with the state of psychoanalytic treatment at the time. Interestingly, the "rediscovery" of Ferenczi's contributions coincided with the recognition of nonverbal communication as a gold mine for analytic inquiry. Subsequently, procedural memory and nonverbal communication have inched their way toward equal partnership with interpretation and verbal communication in psychoanalytic discourse. As a foremost experimenter with psychoanalytic technique, he was also among the first to pursue, if not yet capture, the spirit of inquiry.

Our view that the analyst-patient dialogue is coconstructed includes affect, empathy, and transference in the communications by both analyst and patient. We recognize that in the service of communication with the patient, an analyst utilizes a variety of approaches. These include silence, neutral mirroring, refraining or participating in a transference enactment, explaining, questioning, advice-giving, and reveries and various forms of personal disclosures.

Reveries and disclosures are ubiquitous. A clear distinction between a reverie and empathy and introspection is difficult to make since both engage the analyst's subjectivity and creativity in accessing and conjuring up the experience of the patient. Self-disclosures are a constant, inadvertent by-product of the analyst's engagement in the analytic process, a topic to which we return later in this chapter.

Communication within any dyad is something that each participant is drawn into or repelled by. The conscious and unconscious wishes and needs of each participant will influence the other. Looked at in this way, at one moment silence may be highly desirable, but at another a limited response like "umm" or a fuller mirroring statement or a logical or cognitive explanation or a spontaneous emotional eruption may be called for.

For the purpose of better understanding the analytic process, we can dissect communication into its verbal and nonverbal elements, although a flow between two particular participants, analyst and analysand, remains the essence of the communication. Thus, in this communicative process, we are less justified in describing the virtues and limitations of, for example, listening, umming, explaining, advising, reassuring, encouraging, or interpreting in the abstract, than we are in recognizing how these modes play out. At any particular time, these modes will benefit or inhibit the process in a particular analysis.

To illustrate different forms of communications by the analyst within himself and between him and his patient, a series of sessions from the third year of an analysis follows. The analysis of Nick has been described in other communications (e.g., Lachmann, 2001) although the material that follows has not been previously discussed.

In several sessions from the treatment of Nick (by FL) we illustrate the variety of interventions that contribute toward clarifying, enriching, and broadening the patient-analyst dialogue. We include the analyst's internal monologue-dialogue as an integral part of this process of communication.

Selected sessions from the treatment of Nick illustrate the contribution to therapeutic action of a variety of interpretative and noninterpretive interventions, as well as verbal and nonverbal procedural interactions and enactments. Specifically, in this treatment, the focus was on the transformation of Nick's outbursts of rage and his propensity to withdraw.

Typically, Nick's rage would burst forth when a salesperson in a store was less than competent or efficient, when a coworker was less than cooperative, or when a boss was unreasonably demanding. When, on purchasing an item in a store, he had to wait while the cashier chatted with another salesperson, Nick yelled at her, "You could do the world a favor if you developed terminal cancer!"

Before and during the initial years of our work, Nick's hostile outbursts cost him numerous jobs. This level of rage was not expressed toward me in the course of his analysis except in a somewhat muted form.

When he began analysis, on a three-sessions-a-week basis, Nick was 36 years old. He described himself as despondent and socially quite fearful, with outbursts of self-defeating rage. As Nick spoke in our initial meeting, he cried. He said, "I don't know if I can take care of myself."

Nick is the fourth of five children in a family that lived an economically marginal existence. His father was a quiet, retiring man. His mother appeared to have been severely depressed and frequently nonfunctional.

In his developing years, Nick was very much a loner, both at home and in the outside world. He felt shunned and mocked by his siblings because he was the brightest and because he was unlike the other family members. He increasingly withdrew into a seething, sullen state.

Nick is homosexual. During his adolescence he tried to emulate the heterosexuality of his older brother by playing high school football. Occasionally he dated girls and had sex with some, but he had no sexual interest in them. In college he became actively homosexual.

In his current life, Nick described pervasive feelings of shame, humiliation, anxiety, and rage, which began in his childhood. Scanning the surround became crucial in predicting and avoiding further humiliations. Nick's anxiety often reached extremes in which he experienced himself as rageful and out of control. He felt he could not control his bodily and affect states. Affect states were felt as physical, sexual tensions that he could not regulate, either by containing or expelling his feelings. He felt unable to soothe or enliven himself. These difficulties in self-regulation had led to impulsive rageful behavior.

I found Nick to be emotionally open. His anguish was quite palpable. He had a raucous sense of humor, which occasionally broke through his clouds of despair. At those times I would respond in kind and, for a while, we were able to sustain a playful tone in the session.

The sessions that follow were taken from the third year of Nick's analysis. I believe they were typical and representative of the way in which Nick and I talked with each other. His longing to be accepted by men and his shame at his compliance with his mother's domination were at the center of our sessions. These themes appeared in the transference in that he was often angry at the extent to which he felt dependent on me.

Nick said, "I had a dream Friday night. I felt it strongly on Saturday, like it really happened. Going into the back door of Uncle Joe and Aunt Franny's house. They were not unhappy to see me. Aunt Franny left. I had come to see her. She told Uncle Joe and me to have a good lunch. I hadn't planned on that. She assumed I had come to see Joe and I had actually come to see her. I felt good around him. She was happy to see me, too."

I thought about Aunt Franny turning him over to Uncle Joe and his entering the back door of their house. Imagery and references to anal penetration were relatively easy for Nick to speak about, so I did not think that asking him about this image would lead to new material. During the previous week, however, I had made an error that had enraged him. I had stated that a certain event, a visit from his mother, had occurred on his birthday. It had not. His birthday had been several months earlier. He had been furious at me for forgetting his birthday but also afraid to say so lest I would then not like him. Forgetting the day of his birth had reminded Nick of the numerous ways in which he was "forgotten" in his family. It made me no different from his sister, mother, and all those who failed to inform him of family events. I wondered to what extent his disappointment in my having forgotten his birthday and the thrust of the previous sessions with respect to his ambivalent feelings about his parents were salient in the dream. Referring to Nick's comment that Aunt Franny was happy to see him, I responded with a question, "She was?"

Nick continued in a somewhat lighter tone, "It's unusual for me to visit someone and expect them to be happy to see me. But I was comfortable with their awkwardness, not bothered by it."

In my question, "she was?" I also conveyed to Nick that I was not questioning his account. Was his lighter tone his relief that I had avoided other, more conflicted and painful material? Or was his lighter tone his response to my having passed a test (Weiss and Sampson, 1986), that I had not fallen into a trap and found pathology or criticized as he had anticipated based on his experience in his family? In his response, Nick seemed to address two issues, his appreciation that he was in a family that welcomed him and was "happy to see him," and that their acceptance of him was direct and personal. It did not entail any preconditions, as was the case in his family.

The discomfort of Aunt Franny and Uncle Joe reminded Nick of his own social anxiety. He felt this diminished the distance between him and them. I also thought that my discomfort with having forgotten his birth date may have also assured him that I, too, am subject to feelings of vulnerability, regret, and guilt. To keep his associations going, I mirrored his expressed affect state. I said, "You felt more socially at ease and a comfort that you have longed for."

Nick said, "Yea, the kind of closeness I always wanted in my family. I felt it from Uncle Joe, sometimes. He liked the theater, being gay. He wasn't gay but he could have been."

I sensed an increased comfort with me, implied by his comment about Uncle Joe. Nick now brought up a new theme: the extent to which he felt his homosexuality had isolated him in his family. I had not anticipated this direction. Having kept a low profile until now may well have contributed toward providing the ambience of safety that enabled Nick to proceed in this direction on his own.

I wondered whether Nick might have been referring to his fear of betraying his mother by entering Uncle Joe and Aunt Franny's house through the back door. I also realized that Nick and I might be moving into, and even enacting, a twinship transference. That is, having sensed my vulnerability, Nick now felt more comfortable with me. He concretized his attachment, his shameful dependent attachment, by imagining that Uncle Joe could be gay, and by extension, I assumed, that I could be gay, like him. To let this theme develop further, I said only, "Umumm."

Nick continued, "Uncle Joe and Aunt Franny had a more ideal household world that I wanted. They were always neat. Uncle Joe was interested in intellectual things, reading books, going to plays. They valued the things I wanted. I didn't feel out of place. There was this big incident. The summer after my freshman year at college, I used to go out at night and play tennis with Uncle Joe and Uncle George. Then my sister said that my mother was upset because I was going out every night. I really enjoyed it but I couldn't say 'no' to my mother. I stayed home, that horrid place, watching TV. I wasn't allowed to have contact with my father's family. My aunt was everything that my mother wasn't, and my mother resented her. She insisted that I have the same attitudes as she, and not associate with my father's family, the enemy. I'm angry that I didn't tell my sister to shut the fuck up. I sat around the whole summer doing nothing. I didn't associate with my own friends."

Our dialogue expanded. Although the basic themes in this material were not new—his embarrassment at his mother's disheveled appearance and at the messiness of their home—these details had not been presented before. In addition, there was a new emphasis on the extent of his capitulation to his mother and the extent to which he sacrificed tennis playing with his uncles to TV-watching with his mother. Going through the back door now took on the more specific meaning of avoiding being seen by his mother as he fraternized with her enemies. More generally, he began to distinguish among her views, her expectations that he share them, and his own views. The dream and the associations were presented in a coherent manner and I underscored the dominant message of the dream. I said, "In the dream you defy your mother's 'no.'" I thought of adding, "although you go through the back door" but I decided against this comment since his affect and the spirit of the session were going in another direction: his regret that he had not been more assertive with his mother. That is, he went there on his own. Although I could see the connection between his "back door" image and his regret at his lack of assertion, I was glad I did not lead him to that door but rather followed his lead.

Nick said, "Yeah, doing what I want. Same feeling I had playing tennis. My uncles enjoyed seeing me." Nick continued with wanting to be in a place where he would feel welcomed.

I realized that many transferential themes operated in this dream and his subsequent associations, but I did not know which one to pick up. It seemed to me that Nick was moving tentatively toward a twinship transference and I did not want to steer him away from that. I therefore inquired, "With your uncles you briefly enjoyed feeling valued and that you were wanted. You enjoyed the contact. These are not feelings you usually have about yourself. How come you recalled them now?"

Nick paused for a while and then shifted to numerous familiar topics. He described torturing himself for not working up to his expectations at his job. Then, after another pause, he cried, "I thought more about your not remembering when my birthday is and my reaction to it. I'm pretty enraged. Makes me not want to express that to you. Exposes me as petty. I should be as unconcerned about it as you are. Then I'd be OK. Wouldn't be so nuts as I am. I don't want to talk to you about anything. I don't want to be connected with you. I don't want to be near you, or close to you. I want to find a new shrink I could just hate, one that I wouldn't have to be connected to. Someone I could hate from the outset and not worry about hating them."

Nick returned to my having forgotten the date of his birth, but in a vastly different affective context. He regained a feeling of trust and comfort with me which contributed to his increased self-reflection and as his continuing associations reveal, liberated his sense of humor and his now modulated and transformed aggressive outbursts (Lachmann, 2001). Of course, I recognized the irony in his comment but did not address it. I believed that, had I addressed it, I might have undermined his regained sense of trust and stirred up his ever-present self-criticism. I stayed with his manifest comment, "What makes you worry about hating me?" Nick responded, "Then you'll hate me and then I won't be connected to you," and laughed. I said, "Yeah, that sucks."

Nick laughed, and said, "Therapy is so hard. I want to tell you that and you don't give a shit. You can't even remember my birthday. I want to congratulate myself for going through this and I want you to say it!"

The foregoing interchange captured a slowly evolving procedure in our relationship. Humor, irony, and playful exaggeration characterized our unique personal communication and our connection. From my perspective I disclosed my comfort with, and even liking for, a lighter, playful, even intimate tone. I believe that, from Nick's perspective, he found the kind of "home" in the atmosphere of the sessions that he dreamed about and longed for in his visit to Uncle Joe and Aunt Franny. It was also the kind of atmosphere in which "forgetting" his birthday is not a big deal because, as depicted in his dream, its hurtful impact is ameliorated by his feeling welcomed. In contrast, in his family, being forgotten meant that he was excluded and not wanted. Nick's attachment to me was furthered without his sinking into shame-ridden feelings of dependency that inevitably would lead him into a cycle of self-loathing, rage, and then increased shame. Through our dialogue, which went beyond traditional interpretations, Nick was able to access increasingly more shame-filled memories. Furthermore, in our playfulness we moved toward a twinship transference as well as toward an expansion of the themes that Nick had introduced in the course of the sessions and that he continued in the subsequent sessions.

When Nick lay on the couch, he faced one of my bookcases, the one that held my copies of *The Psychoanalytic Quarterly*. The theme of his shame at his ready capitulation to his mother led to his feelings of shame about his sexual curiosity. At the same time his connection to me remained a central issue. With his concern about his sexuality he wondered what I do in my office when I'm alone. He spoke of his "jerking off" and imagined me in my bathroom "jerking off with *The Psychoanalytic Quarterly.*" I said, "Oh, you mean because it has all those pictures?" I deliberately did not want to pathologize his "fantasy."

I assume that Nick's humor with me as well as mine with him, as in our comments about my use of *The Psychoanalytic Quarterly*, was coconstructed. My respect for and enjoyment of Nick's humor and his expectation that we might play with it, I believe, enabled Nick to make that comment. From other therapeutic approaches a response to the literal meaning and analysis of his fantasy might have been offered. For example, challenging: "what makes you think that I jerk off?" or confronting: "depicting me with *The Psychoanalytic Quarterly* in this way, is a derogatory way of describing me and my work, what is that about?" Even, at this point, interpreting "you want to make me similar to you" might have been a betrayal of the spirit of our ongoing communication. I would have suddenly left my somewhat ambiguous position in a "play space" with Nick and differentiated and distinguished myself as the *analyst.*

The various interventions I just described constitute inquiries with an agenda or an authoritarian edge. They are not conducted in the spirit of further understanding, rather they impart an opinion and criticism without so stating. But, most important, they delineate a gulf between therapist and patient. Such a difference is of course always present. It is at best in the background, especially at times when the patient, for compelling developmental purposes, is striving to establish a twinship transference. It seemed to me that this was the direction in which Nick and I were moving. At such times, the therapist can succumb to the danger of sending the patient a metacommunication: we are *not* alike and it is hostile on your part to depict us as fellow masturbators. We would thereby have been repeating in the analysis just the kind of experience of shame, rage, and social isolation that Nick lived through in his family. We would have been repeating in the analysis what Ferenczi (1933) described as "professional hypocrisy" (p. 159), no different from the hypocrisy that prevailed in his family that was implicated in the organization of his dread, "I don't know if I can take care of myself." To this dread we could now add, "I don't believe anyone else would care about me unless I comply with what they want of me."

In the subsequent session, Nick expressed his curiosity about his parents' sexual life. He had felt convinced that they never had sexual relations. He then wondered when my birthday was which I explained as his curiosity as to when *my* parents had sex. In contrast to his preoccupation with sex, he had believed that his parents were asexual and he was now investigating this issue with respect to my parents and, I thought, ultimately with me. I now interpreted to him that his imagining that we both jerked off was his way of making a connection with me in a way that had felt shameful. He was daring to find similarities between us. I added that it seemed important to him that sexuality occupies similar places in our lives. It made him feel connected with me, less different, less alone.

Although I had refrained from making such interpretations earlier lest they sound injurious and potentially pathologize his sexual feelings, I believe that eventually such interpretations are necessary. They addressed his pervasive sense of shame about his sexuality. For Nick and me to have a twinship transference based on a shared feeling of shame about sexuality would not have furthered the treatment.

Nick's analysis lasted 11 years. The themes outlined in the sessions from the third year of his analysis, as well as other issues having to do with his difficulties in self-regulation of affect and arousal dominated much of the analysis.

After termination of the analysis, Nick wrote me a letter in which he analyzed an element from his last dream. In it he depicted a woman toward whom he did not behave so compliantly. His dream contained an image of a woman picking his pocket in a police station. He wrote that she "was not inside me. I realize of course that the contents of the dream are all, in a sense, inside me. But what the dream was showing was this women outside of me, not internalized. She was separate. Yes, she still tries to cling to me, attempting to grab what is mine when I'm not paying attention. However, she's clearly seen as a separate person. It's also clear to me what's mine—and not hers. She is separate from me without my having to destroy her, which of course has long been the only alternative I considered possible (doing damage mostly to myself in the process).

"This realization made me feel very happy and added to the confidence I feel about what and who I am and what I possess. This woman is still a problem in the dream. I have to be vigilant to keep what's mine. But she's become more the nuisance, than the threat to existence she had been (or so it seemed to me). She's like traffic in the big city—an annoyance but not the defining element of life. And, like traffic, the police do little to solve the problem. Just thought you might enjoy hearing these additional thoughts."

I enjoyed the touch of irony in his dream, that the woman "is like traffic in the big city." In addition, his last comment reflected the extent to which our connection still held and to his benefit. He could reflect on his dream with a sense of pleasure and curiosity.

As a whole, the portion of Nick's analysis that has been presented illustrates the ebb and flow of our interactions, our process. Nick's expectations that he would be abandoned and shunned unless he behaved compliantly were gradually disconfirmed. Continued attention throughout his analysis to his propensity to withdraw angrily, increased the range and flexibility of his participation. His complaints about whether or not I cared about him became less intense and somewhat less frequent.

Nick's participation in the process of treatment tilted the therapeutic process toward repetition of patterns that were familiar to him, specifically rageful compliance. However, my presence challenged this repetition. From a systems perspective, it provided a "perturbation" to our interaction (Thelen and Smith, 1994). Thus, the therapeutic process could move away from following his longstanding expectations, familiar experiences of feeling criticized and in danger of abandonment and humiliation if he did not produce or comply.

The way in which Nick and I spoke and listened to each other attests to the inseparability of self and interactive regulation. Clearly Nick and I each had a preformed mode of communication, unique and personal, like a fingerprint, which we brought to the analysis. In addition, we learned how to adapt to each other in the course of the sessions. In the background of our interplay was our joint spirit of inquiry, a desired mutual expansion of consciousness (Tronick et al., 1998). I varied my participation although, at any given moment that participation was more often preconscious rather than deliberate and thought through. Many of my interventions were thought about prior to my offering them, but my playfulness and humor were spontaneous. I was cognizant of a necessary "discipline" to my interventions. I did not want to "upstage" Nick or turn the treatment into a showcase for my humor. On the other hand, I would not want to be party to a dry, pedantic exercise that sometimes passes for a "good" analysis.

When the analyst departs from the "patient-talks–analyst-listens-and-interprets" model, the therapeutic ambience can certainly on occasion be lighter. However, when the windows of the analytic consulting room are opened to fresh air, sometimes a moth or mosquito can fly in. It is for this reason that we (Lichtenberg, Lachmann, and Fosshage, 1992) have written about "disciplined spontaneous engagements."

I have always kept in mind a patient of Ralph Greenson's (1970) who dreamed that he was in a clothing store in which he wanted clothes that were "tailor made." He complained to Greenson that he received from him interpretations that were pulled off the "ready-to-wear" rack. The intervention I made to Nick's "masturbating with the *Psychoanalytic Quarterly*" was "tailor made" just for him. At those moments he signaled his readiness for "something more" (Stern et al., 1998) by shifting to a directly challenging and metaphoric form of communication. I joined his readiness for further transformative rather than repetitive experiences. He felt more capable of taking care of himself, which reflected his increased confidence in his self-regulation in the context of our interaction.

Although the entire treatment was conducted in a spirit of inquiry, there were specific inquiring moments in the course of the session. As for example, my question, "she was?" about being welcomed by Aunt Franny. Even in this two word question, affect and intonation convey important information about our relationship. This was also true of the occasional silences and umms that characterized the flow of our dialogue. These were times when I not only wanted to give Nick the opportunity to expand on what he had been saying, but I also needed the breathing space to organize and clarify my own understanding, and to sense the direction into which Nick and I were moving.

The flow of the sessions was maintained, primarily, by an ambience of safety that Nick and I had constructed. Nick felt that I clearly was determined to understand him in the context of his life. As best I could, I conveyed to Nick that I did not fear being linked or connected to him, or that conversely, I needed to distance myself from him to protect myself or my analytic persona.

In describing these sessions, it is easier to do so with respect to our verbal interactions than along a nonverbal dimension. The two most obvious nonverbal, affective communications were Nick's crying when he spoke about his worry that he would not be able to take care of himself, and our shared laughter. In the first instance, I was certainly moved, but not to tears. I remained silent for a while and then acknowledged his concern and that we would be addressing it over the course of his treatment. But, when we laughed, we laughed together.

Pauses in the course of a session were opportunities to switch (or not to switch) to a new track. When Nick paused after I inquired how it was that he recalled his pleasure at being welcomed by his uncle, he moved into a new area. My silence at that time reflected my appreciation of Nick's private struggle. This enabled him to find his own way through his material. I think this illustrated a judicious use of my silence. In contrast, in an earlier session when Nick had spoken about a visit from his mother, silence, rather than trying to place that visit on his birthday, would have been more judicious.

When I reflected on this lapse of mine at a later time, I thought that I may have been pushing for greater intimacy than was called for. I think I was trying too hard to show Nick how well I knew him. I did not reveal this to Nick since a relevant transference configuration "you are like my family who forget me" had been organized. When it comes to self-disclosures, I have no difficulty in disclosing my style, humor, even a variety of interests, but my personal motives are another matter. Often they can be inferred from the interaction, but what I have just revealed in my write-up, I am unlikely to include in the treatment. I believe it is often difficult to ascertain the therapeutic necessity of an analyst's self-disclosure. Is a fair depiction of the analyst's private world, crucial for the progress of the treatment, specifically required to extricate the treatment from a stalemate? Or, is the self-disclosure by the analyst self-serving, self-promoting, or self-aggrandizing? Is it offered to further the spirit of inquiry or does it cut off inquiry into aspects of the transference that the analyst prefers to circumvent?

In the interpretive sequence in response to Nick's dream about his visit to Aunt Franny and Uncle Joe, I interpreted the leading edge (Lachmann, 2001; Miller, 1985; Tolpin, 2001) what Nick was attempting to achieve. Through this intervention Nick apparently felt safe enough to venture into a new area. In addition, in this instance, I refrained from offering a trailing edge interpretation, what Nick was defending against, the back-door reference. In retrospect this was a good idea since Nick proceeded productively in that direction on his own. Whether or not a trailing edge interpretation would have temporarily closed off further inquiry and associations, cannot be known. However, I believe that such trailing edge interpretations, when ill timed, can lead to transference enactments that repeat the shaming and humiliating experiences that marked Nick's childhood.

There has been an accumulation of analytic literature on the myth of neutrality. Silence, ummumming, or mirroring are all open to a wide range of meanings. They are co-constructed and open to a variety of interpretations on the part of the patient (or, from the analyst's perspective, sometimes misinterpretations). In essence, all of these responses are designed to keep the patient's communications going. In the sessions presented these interpretations all appear but certainly not repetitively. Although designed to keep the session going with a minimal, suggestive influence from the analyst, their accumulation in a session will have an impact of its own. In the session presented, these interventions were all used at a time when Nick was working on material and searching for a direction to pursue. I would not use them as such if I felt Nick was stuck, unsure of where to go, or waiting for a response or signal from me. At such times rather than remain silent, I have told Nick that I agree that a response on my part would be helpful here, but I do not yet feel clear about what to offer. Such responses, in lieu of literal and injudicious silence on the part of the analyst, enables the patient to continue his or her work, without the additional burden of feeling that the analyst is using silence as a "technique."

To participate or not to participate in a transference enactment is the analytic counterpart to Hamlet's question. It is probably rarely resolved on a conscious level. However, cognition contributes to the analyst's choices to restrain or to energize the treatment. In my intervention to Nick, "because it has all those pictures," I simultaneously did and did not engage in a twinship transference enactment. We were twin humorists if not necessarily twin masturbators. These two sets of twins are not identical, but it was close enough. The enactment constituted an unverbalized bond, an intimacy. It expressed my readiness to be engaged on a personal level with Nick, and his readiness to relinquish his tendency toward trigger-like, rageful withdrawal.

There are probably more frequent occurrences of spontaneous emotional eruptions on the part of analysts in the course of treatments than the published analytic literature reflects. In my "yeah that sucks" response, I joined Nick's dilemma that he wanted to hate me but couldn't because if he did, I would not be connected to him. This dilemma, although presented with humor, was quite real for him. My joining him in the humorous contradiction acknowledged the horns of the dilemma on which he was caught without trivializing it. I believe that this interaction constituted another instance which furthered our connection without making him self-conscious. In these instances, the analyst can participate in an enactment, avoid participation by interpreting the patient's wish to draw the analyst into an enactment, or describe the process and these two options to the patient. When the analyst tries to avoid being drawn into an enactment, he or she may well be drawn into another kind of enactment: a playful, fun-loving, teasing patient with a sourfaced, spoilsport analyst.

If the model "patient talks, analyst listens and interprets" is rigidly adhered to, then that danger of repeating the original trauma in the analysis is ever present. The analyst will then appear to be similar to an unresponsive or uncaring caretaker. However, if the treatment moves too far in the direction of a friendly relationship then the danger is that analyst and patient have a good relationship that is so different from the patient's original experience that the patient's childhood is essentially left intact outside of the treatment. Moreover, the joint pursuit of analytic understanding can be diminished. These are the Scylla and Charybdis that the analyst negotiates in this process. And to engage in such a complex navigation, a number of variations of the traditional analytic intervention model are required. For this reason a modicum of enactments is crucial for the analysis to be alive and to capture relevant childhood experiences. A process of open flexible communication such as this produces the alterations of rough seas and smooth voyages that characterized this treatment, and that characterize treatments so frequently.

CHAPTER FOUR

EFFECTIVE COMMUNICATIVE EXCHANGES

As we delineated in chapters 1 and 2, communicative exchanges between the developing child and caregiver are complex interactions involving a wide range of verbal and nonverbal expressions. In chapter 3, we illustrated that the psychoanalytic enterprise is no different. Open, flexible communicative exchanges between patient and analyst involve finely nuanced reading of one another similar to those between parent and child and between adults. In this chapter, we focus on various contemporary theories of change within the psychoanalytic encounter that draw on developmental, cognitive, and neuroscientific research, as well as on psychoanalytic theory and clinical experience. We explore the effectiveness of communicative exchanges from the standpoint of implicit/nondeclarative and explicit/declarative domains; the intractability of pathological mental models; the analyst's affective participation; and, forms of relatedness. In addition to verbal/affective interactions, we include a consideration of physical touch and its use as a form of communication. We believe that understanding emerging within these areas increases our understanding of processes of change and enhances the communicative exchange.

Whether an analyst's understanding of therapeutic action is focused on interpretation/insight or relational experience, communication can be regarded as central in that both interpretation and relating are communicative experiences. Communicative exchanges, however, are shaped significantly by the analyst's model of therapeutic action. Freud initially thought that rendering the unconscious conscious was central for change and, with that goal in mind, developed the technique of asking the patient to associate as freely as possible. The analyst's principle communication became that of interpretation, to make the unconscious conscious, to engender insight. Interpretation focused principally on the revelation of intrapsychic dynamics, unconscious wishes and fantasies, and emphasizing the recovery of the repressed. The analyst delivered interpretations as an objective, neutral observer without affective participation.

Freud, however, was on occasion even more convinced of the importance of the relationship as promoting psychoanalytic change (Friedman, 1978). In 1916 Freud said, "What turns the scale is not intellectual insight, but the relationship to the doctor" (p. 445); and in 1937, the analyst must be a "model" as well as a "teacher" (p. 248). In keeping with this emphasis, Ferenczi and those psychoanalysts who followed him focused on the relational experience as central to therapeutic change. Spearheaded by Ferenczi, they asserted that "the physician's love heals the patient." Emphasizing love (Suttie, 1935; Balint, 1952, 1968), the holding environment (Winnicott, 1965), new object experience (Loewald, 1960), and mirroring and idealizing selfobject transferences (Kohut, 1971, 1977, 1984) broadened the range and focus of the analyst's responses far beyond interpretation of intrapsychic dynamics and powerfully affected the communicative exchange.

With further developments in psychoanalysis such as the emergence of intersubjective or relational theory (Atwood and Stolorow, 1984; Stolorow, Brandchaft, and Atwood, 1987; Mitchell, 1988, 1993), the content of interpretations has come to focus on past and current relational experience, expectancies, organizing schemas, and constructions that could be either repressed or were never subject to conscious reflection. A relational or systems perspective views patient and analyst interacting, communicating, and mutually influencing one another (Beebe, Jaffe, and Lachmann, 1992), creating an "intersection of two subjectivities" (Stolorow, Brandchaft, and Atwood, 1987). From this perspective, interpretation, understanding, and the totality of the patient-analyst relationship become more inextricably intertwined. That is, understanding emerges within and is affected by the analyst/patient relationship; creating a full circle, the relationship is affected by understanding. In relational theory, the goal shifts to a therapeutic interaction as opposed to the singular pursuit of insight (Renik, 1998). The communicative exchange, from a systems perspective, becomes far more complex (Lichtenberg, 1999).

Over the past century, the different psychoanalytic models of development and therapeutic action have, thus, powerfully reshaped the process and content of communicative exchanges. Mitchell (1988) synthesized the various theories into three perspectives: the drive-conflict model, the deficiency-compensation model, and the relational-conflict model. Correspondingly, Stark (1999) boiled down the therapeutic action of these models respectively to "enhancement of knowledge, provision of experience, [and] engagement in relationship" (p. xv). These agents of change, in our view, are not separate processes, but are different aspects of analysts' interventions. One aspect or another comes to the foreground, affected by the analyst's models and the moment-to-moment communicative exchange. The foreground/background shifts account for substantially different interventions. From a systems perspective, to interpret and enhance knowledge provides a particular kind of experience, emerging out of a particular kind of relational engagement. Directly or indirectly to acknowledge, affirm, validate, or soothe (provision) is a particular kind of relational experience that also enhances knowledge (implicitly, explicitly or both). A mutual recognition by analyst and analysand of each other's subjectivity (Benjamin, 1990) constitutes, moreover, a particular kind of relational engagement that enhances knowledge (implicitly, explicitly, or both). We propose that *the spirit of inquiry* embraces all three aspects of interventions as they shift from the foreground to the background and serves as the fundamental underpinning of the psychoanalytic process.

How does psychological change occur? What communicative exchanges are effective in promoting change within the psychoanalytic arena? These are fundamental questions that, from the beginning, psychoanalysts have grappled with. As part of our efforts to address these questions, our first two books focused on conceptual and technical guidelines from a self- and motivational systems perspective, while this book focuses specifically on communication and the spirit of inquiry.

Implicit/Nondeclarative and Explicit/Declarative Domains

The recent efforts to integrate cognitive science and psychoanalytic models of development and change have significant implications for the communicative exchange (e.g., Clyman, 1991; Modell, 1994; Bucci, 1997; Stern et al., 1998; Fishman, 1999; Fonagy, 1999; Westen, 1999; Davis, 2001). Cognitive science models differentiate between two domains of knowledge and memory—implicit/nondeclarative and explicit/declarative. The terms implicit and explicit refer to whether or not memory can be consciously recollected or not (Davis, 2001). The term declarative memory (Cohen and Squire, 1980) refers to a memory system involved in the processing of information that an individual can consciously recall and *"declare* to remember" (Davis, 2001, p. 451). Cohen and Squire (1980) originally differentiated between declarative and procedural memory. Squire (1994) subsequently came to view procedural memory as one type of nondeclarative memory, the latter consisting of several separate memory systems. The nondeclarative memory systems influence experience and behavior, but cannot be explicitly or consciously recalled. Davis (2001) describes how classical conditioning and skill-and-habit memory are two nondeclarative memory systems. Classical conditioning is now viewed as "a 'high-level' process capable of representing complex temporal, spatial and logical relations between events, features of those events, and the contexts in which the events occur . . . [and] form the primary basis for an organism's expectations about the nature of future events" (p. 452). Skills and habits are learned either consciously or unconsciously, and through gradual incremental learning (Schacter and Tulving, 1994) become automatic procedures. LeDoux (1996) distinguishes between emotional memory and the declarative memory of an emotional situation. Declarative memory entails facts of the situation; emotional memory refers to emotional responses during the event.

In their dynamic systems model of developmental change applied to the understanding of psychoanalytic change, Stern et al. (1998), integrating cognitive science, delineate between "the declarative, or conscious verbal, domain; and the implicit procedural or *relational* domain" (p. 904). They differentiate between explicit (declarative) and implicit (procedural) knowledge, memory, and representations that are constructed and reorganized in psychoanalysis. While procedural knowledge of relationships is represented nonsymbolically in the form of what they call *implicit relational knowing*, such knowing can either remain out of awareness or serve as the basis for symbolical representation in imagistic or verbal form. They write:

> In summary, declarative knowledge is gained or acquired through verbal interpretations that alter the patient's intrapsychic understanding within the context of the "psychoanalytic," and usually transferential, relationship. *Implicit relational knowing*, on the other hand, occurs through "interactional, intersubjective processes" that alter the relational field within the context of what we will call the "shared implicit relationship" [p. 905].

Implicit (procedural) relational knowledge corresponds with "the representational world" (Sandler and Rosenblatt, 1962), "internal working models" (Bowlby, 1973), "patterns of organization" (Wachtel, 1980; Stolorow and Lachmann, 1984/1985; Fosshage, 1994), "RIGs or representations of interactions that are generalized" (Stern, 1985), "pathogenic beliefs" (Weiss and Sampson, 1986), "mental representations" (Fonagy, 1993), "interactional structures" (Beebe and Lachmann, 1994), "expectancies"

(Lichtenberg, Lachmann, and Fosshage, 1996), and "themes of organization" (Sander, 1997). Implicit mental models develop unconsciously, what Stolorow and Atwood (1992) call the pre-reflective unconscious, and organize and construct life experience through expectancies, selective attention, attribution of meanings, and interpersonal construction (Fosshage, 1994). Implicit mental models vary along a number of dimensions, such as frequency of use, modifiability, and availability to consciousness (Fosshage, 1994). For our purposes, we use interchangeably the terms implicit mental models, implicit relational knowing, patterns of organization, schemas, and expectancies.

As part of the interactional, intersubjective processes, Stern et al. (1998) describe "now moments" as affectively "hot" moments that require "a response that is too specific and personal to be a known technical manoeuvre. . . . They force the therapist into some kind of 'action,' be it an interpretation or a response that is novel relative to the habitual framework, or a silence"(p. 911). A now moment therapeutically seized is a "moment of meeting" which they describe:

> The two are meeting as persons relatively unhidden by their usual therapeutic roles, for that moment. Also, the actions that make up the "moment of meeting" cannot be routine, habitual accessibility to or technical; they must be novel and fashioned to meet the singularity of the moment. Of course this implies a measure of empathy, an openness to affective and cognitive reappraisal, a signalled affect attunement, a viewpoint that reflects and ratifies that what is happening is occurring in the domain of the "shared implicit relationship," i.e., a newly created dyadic state specific to the participants [p. 913].

Moments of meeting, we suggest, may also occur quite spontaneously and unexpectedly. A number of years ago, for example, I (JLF) saw for the first time a young woman who had just completed social work training. She mentioned in the first session that she was going for a job interview later that afternoon. During a pause in the next session, I spontaneously inquired about the job interview. The patient immediately broke into tears, saying with considerable pain and relief that her father, a very self-involved man, would never have asked her about her job interview. This "moment of meeting" involved two people authentically engaged. From the patient's perspective, we communicated in a new way (new implicit and explicit knowledge) that unexpectedly countered her implicit relational knowledge. Juxtaposition of her expectancies with our, to her, unexpected interaction helped to bring the implicit relational knowledge more sharply into conscious (explicit) focus.

Stern et al. (1998) suggest that "interpretations can lead to 'moments of meeting' or the other way around. . . . If the interpretation is made in a way that conveys the affective participation of the analyst, a 'moment of meeting' may also have occurred" (p. 914). The analyst must be affectively engaged so as to reveal "a personal aspect of the self that has been evoked in an affective response to another" (p. 917). Moments of meeting act "within and upon the 'shared implicit relationship' and change it by altering implicit knowledge that is both intrapsychic and interpersonal" (p. 917). Stern et al. declare that longlasting change occurs in the domain of implicit relational knowledge. "In the course of the analysis some of the implicit relational knowledge will get slowly and painstakingly transcribed into conscious explicit knowledge. How much is an open question" (p. 918).

How the implicit/nondeclarative and explicit/declarative cognitive domains interact is centrally important in the consideration of effecting change within the psychoanalytic arena. The interaction between these two domains is not clear. However, additional findings about memory that integrate cognitive and neuroscientific research are becoming available.

In the broadest definition, "memory is the way past events affect future function" (Siegel, 1999, p. 24). The firing of a neural circuitry, a "neural net profile," increases the probability of it being reactivated in the future. Hebb's law (1949) is: Neurons that fire together wire together. "The increased probability of firing a similar pattern is how the network 'remembers'" (p. 24).

(Neural net profiles are also called neural memory networks or maps [Nelson, 1986; Edelman, 1987; Levin, 1991].) Whereas transient metabolic changes are involved in short-term memory, more stable structural changes are involved in long-term memory. Importantly, repetition of firings and the involvement of affect increase the probability that the neural net profile will become engrained circuits of the brain and will enter long-term memory storage. Based on infant research, neural nets are established, in the language of Beebe and Lachmann (1994), through ongoing regulatory interactions and heightened affect.

The implicit memory system is devoid of a subjective experience of recalling and does not require focal attention for encoding. Registration of information subliminally and procedural memories are part of the implicit memory system. The implicit memory system is operative at birth. In contrast, the explicit memory system is understood to require conscious focal attention for encoding and has a subjective sense of recollection. It involves the memory of facts (semantic) and episodes (for example, autobiographical or oneself in an episode of time). While implicit capacity develops very early in life; explicit capacity develops during the second year of life. *Implicit mental models* shape the explicit autobiography (in other language, organizing patterns affect our conscious perceptions). Long-term memory items become a part of permanent explicit memory through a process called "cortical consolidation," a process that is not well understood, but may require REM sleep for consolidation (Siegel, 1999, p. 37). Narratives about who we are emerge as value-laden memories that are consolidated into the permanent explicit autobiographical system.

Our sense of self is derived from both memory systems. Explicit memory cues evoke implicit memories, and implicit mental models affect explicit memory. Siegel notes: "Our internal sense of who we are is shaped both by what we can explicitly recall, and by the implicit recollections that create our mental models and internal subjective experience of images, sensations, emotions, and behavioral responses" (p. 46). When explicit and implicit autobiographical memories are consonant, a person experiences an increased sense of self-cohesion (independent of negative or positive valence). Research of trauma victims demonstrates that individuals who dissociate explicit and implicit processing in autobiographical memory in response to trauma are most vulnerable to posttraumatic stress disorder.

When guided by *a spirit of inquiry*, verbal and nonverbal psychoanalytic exchanges highlight both the autobiographical scenarios of explicit memory and the mental models of implicit memory as each memory system contributes to a sense of self, other, and self with other. *An analyst's and patient's affective coparticipation in the striving to explore, understand and communicate understanding creates an interaction that contributes, through gradual incremental learning, to new implicit relational knowledge.* The spirit of inquiry that guides this implicit relational interaction, is a cornerstone of an analytic process, as well as a crucial component of other vital human relationships. *The "inquiry" brings explicit/declarative processing to the foreground in the striving to explore, understand and communicate.* Bringing declarative focus to the situation, usually, not always, tends to highlight the old mental models and reinforce new implicit relational knowledge. When we say "not always," we are referring to those situations that need to be "lived in," where focused attention disrupts the affective moment, the "moment of meeting," and is only facilitative at a later time. Whether immediately or later, focused attention on new procedural interactive experience may not be necessary or possible, but tends to facilitate integration of the experience and the establishment of new corresponding models in both memory systems.

In the ordinary course of analytic work a current perceptual/affective experience is assimilated into previously established networks for categorization and further attribution of meaning. New experience for which no category or neural memory network exists is registered in immediate memory, but tends to have difficulty in entering long-term memory. Explicit highlighting of an old implicit mental model that stands out in relief when juxtaposed with a new model, creates a conscious perspective that aids in the deactivation of the old. Deactivation of an old mental model facilitates integration of new implicit relational knowledge and corresponding explicit knowledge into long-term memory, gradually consolidated in permanent memory. When an old traumatic theme (implicit relational knowledge) is replicated in the analytic relationship, focused attention enables analyst and analysand to observe, understand, and extricate themselves from the replication, creating new implicit relational experience.

We agree with Stern et al. (1998) that "moments of meeting" are necessary to impact the domain of implicit relational knowledge. A moment of meeting will have a dynamic relational impact, but for it to have an analytically transformative impact, the moment of meeting must be embedded in a relationship implicitly and explicitly guided by a spirit of inquiry. An analyst striving to explore, understand and communicate generates new implicit relational knowledge and brings focused attention on implicit mental models and explicit autobiographical narratives. The implicit in the "spirit" and the explicit in the "inquiry" involve both processing and memory systems in effecting psychoanalytic change. We see the foreground/background shifting between the implicit and explicit domains as an interactional dance within the psychoanalytic arena, each aiding and abetting the other so long as the toes of neither are stepped on.

Intractability of Mental Models

Why are mental models so immutable? This is of particular concern to psychoanalysts when negative mental models, involving, for example, negative (devitalizing) self percepts, persist despite contrary relational experience.

Cogent psychoanalytic explanations have included that aspects of an unconscious conflict have not yet become conscious (drive/conflict model), that the patient is holding onto a bad object (object relations theory), that the patient is maintaining a needed selfobject tie (self psychology), and that the patient is employing whatever strategy he or she formed to adhere to a secure base (attachment theory). Any one of these dynamic formulations might lend explanatory value to a particular experience. In our view, why negative mental models are so resistant to change emerges out of the function of the implicit/nondeclarative memory system. That is, *implicit mental models serve a primary adaptive function*. Lived experience establishes expectancies that enable us to anticipate, interpret and interact with the world for purposes of negotiation and survival (attachment theorists, see Main, 2000). Experience of the world that is discrepant with expectancies is disruptive and challenges current views of reality. These disruptions jeopardize self-cohesion, self-regulation and capacity to negotiate. While organizing activity is infinitely complex so that many patterns remain flexible and acceptable to accommodation, primary organizing patterns can become relatively "invariant" (Stolorow, Brandchaft, and Atwood, 1987). Their invariance is related psychologically to their adaptive value, that is, the continued relative cogency of the strategy being employed, cognitively to their long-term or permanent implicit and explicit memory status, and neurologically to the establishment of primary (increased probability of firing) neural memory networks. Correspondingly, Davis (2001) suggests that "the resistance to change" of the "patient's expectations and emotional inhibitions reflects the fact that his early relationship dynamic with his parents is additionally represented in non-declarative classically conditioned associations" (p. 454).

A clinical illustration follows that involves inquiry, reflection, and recollection of a declarative and nondeclarative (emotional) memory. Furthermore, the repetition of new implicit and explicit relational experience is described. These experiences, involving heightened affect, were used to overcome the iron grip of negative self and self-with-other percepts. Susan, in her mid 40s, was the firstborn of seven children. The core trauma was captured in a model scene (Lichtenberg, Lachmann, and Fosshage, 1992) in which Susan, as a little girl, stands at the doorway, wanting and hoping but afraid to ask for attention from her father who is sitting and reading the newspaper. She recalled moments of intense closeness with her father, sitting and cuddling on his lap; yet, her father, more often, was experienced as self-preoccupied and noncommunicative. In addition, he had an unpredictably explosive temper. The birth of her first sibling, a sister, when she was six, apparently captivated her father's attention, leaving her feeling "displaced" from her father's lap and rendered invisible. Susan's mother was not experienced as emotionally "present." As her other siblings arrived, Susan found her mother to be increasingly unavailable and unrelated to her children, frequently confusing their names. In contrast, she experienced her grandmother who spoke in a language foreign to her to be the one consistently affirming and comforting person. Her grandmother would express her love and caring through facial expressions and physical touch. Susan valiantly fought to establish and maintain self-esteem, against easily triggered devastating feelings of rejection and humiliation. She became a caretaker of her siblings, a model student, excelled academically, and was personally well liked. As an adult, with the same battle waging in her, she expressed and maintained her vitality through her efforts as a wife, mother, friend, and professional. Despite considerable success in her endeavors, the trauma of devaluation, rejection, and humiliation was always close at hand.

Prior to the current analysis, Susan had experienced a long analytic treatment with an analyst who had precipitously terminated her analysis. He claimed that she was impossible to help and, thereby, replicated the trauma of her parents' rejection of her once again. Six months later she began analysis with me (JLF) face to face, three times a week. The focus for the first year of analysis was to understand and find a way through the trauma that was created by the termination of the first analysis. Gradually as she reemerged from the trauma, she was able to focus more directly on her current analytic experience. She risked allowing mirroring and idealizing selfobject needs to emerge once again in an analytic relationship. In the third year of the analysis Susan joined an analytic group that I led.

Susan longed for my affirmation and wanted to feel "special," in the sense of feeling valued, unique, and important in my eyes. Yet, she was convinced that she was not special or valued and, though she felt I liked her, she felt that I did not really see or respond to her as special. I was aware of my increasing fondness for her. Yet, to the degree that she remained protectively hidden (in response to her expectation of rejection), I felt that I could not see or respond to her sufficiently for us to be able to establish a sense of feeling valued. This relational configuration tended to confirm, yet again, her negative percepts. Exploration and interpretive understanding of this relational scenario helped us to begin to extricate ourselves from it. She began, on occasion, to express herself with fuller affect that fostered reciprocally increased affective intensity in my responses. I, in turn, became more active in my inquiry—for example, shortening the length of silences between us, increasing my affective expression. My increased activity reciprocally increased Susan's expressiveness. Thus, our engagement gradually deepened, including an emergent mutually reciprocal feeling that I "knew" her and valued her.

This emergent bond intensified through an interplay of empathic understanding and my more direct communication of affirmation through words, vocal tonality, facial expressions, and physical touch. Touch involved the brief placement of my hand on her shoulder as she was walking out the door, a playful light kicking of her shoe on occasion during the session, and, later, an occasional hug at the door as she was leaving the session (the issue of touch in this analysis will be addressed as the final topic of this chapter).

Despite an intense mirroring and idealizing selfobject bond, the negative percepts of her devalued sense of self and of the analyst as insufficiently valuing of her were readily triggered by my inadvertent contributions and Susan's constructions. When her traumatic self-with-other configuration, riveted with shame and deflation, was activated, Susan needed me to stay with her in the trauma, to make certain that I heard and understood her traumatic feelings of rejection. She needed desperately not to be left alone in her traumatic state, as she had experienced in the past with her parents. She also needed me to acknowledge my contribution to her experience. Otherwise, how could she know that I understood my contribution, could possibly change, and not repeat it again? I gradually learned that when I moved too quickly from focusing on my contribution to her constructions (including both when I was defensive or simply overly analytically ambitious), Susan would experience me as not "getting it" and "blaming her." This, in turn, intensified her hopelessness about impacting me. When she felt that I really "got it," she would gradually become more aware of her particular constructions and how they resonated with traumatic themes of the past. Thus, we moved from the old percepts to the new, and back again.

In analytic group therapy, Susan not infrequently complained that I did not attend to her as much as to the other members in the group. As Susan and I carefully tracked these occasions, we realized that Susan's hesitancy to speak in the group was not always clear to me. At times she would meaningfully comment, but without sending a clear enough message for the group members or me to understand that she wanted to be invited to say more. Misreading her, the group and I would not pursue her and she would end up feeling devalued and unimportant. Susan was like the little girl at the door wanting her analyst's (and group's) attention and hesitant to express it for fear of rejection, and I was "too busy with the newspaper to notice." Her complaint to me was an instance of speaking out, of expressing and asserting herself more fully. I emphasized that we needed to work together to be able to create the needed experience. That is, I needed to listen more carefully and she needed to let me know, as best she could, that she wanted to say more or wanted more from me, or was having difficulty doing either.

In the individual session just prior to a crucial incident in the analytic group, Susan was feeling particularly pleased and alive, partially because I had spontaneously made what turned out to be a facilitative suggestion for her in dealing with a work situation. She felt valued and cared for. Later that evening in analytic group, another member spoke. I could see deflation in Susan setting in and inquired about what was happening. Together, and with the group, we were able to identify that the member getting "air time" was triggering in Susan the old negative percepts that she did not count. She anticipated that I, as her mother, could not see the children as individuals and recognize each in his or her own right and that I, as her father, was "taken" with her sibling, leaving her feeling invisible. With a powerful gravitational pull, the old percepts were taking over and an explicit/declarative analytic focus was proving to be of no help. This was not the emergence of the repressed, for Susan was all too familiar with it. Rather it was the reactivation of repetitive, devitalizing percepts (implicit mental models). Exploration and interpretation were ineffective. Although I was attentive and engaged with Susan, I could do nothing to stop the deteriorating process. I then spontaneously asked if she could remember what she had been feeling in the previous individual session and if she could tell the group about it. As Susan was able gradually to remember how she had felt valued and cared for and expressed it in the group, with the group serving as a fortifying witness, the process strikingly enabled Susan to reclaim her new percepts and to deactivate the old. As she spoke, her vitality returned. She was able to focus on and regain contact with her more recent declarative and emotional memories (LeDoux, 1996) involving a vitalizing connection between her and her analyst. At the interactional level of implicit relational knowing, my question implicitly reconfirmed, now within the group, her new vitalizing percepts and facilitated her reconnecting with them. At that moment, Susan and I had achieved a way of being together in the group that enabled her to feel valued and special. While these new percepts were initially momentary and episodic, alternating with the older configurations, gradually they began to be expanded with deepened emotional conviction in time and memory.

The Analyst's Affective Participation

Over the past 25 years a remarkable change has been taking place within psychoanalysis. First, eschewing our position of objectivity, no longer viable in light of the paradigmatic change from positivistic to relativistic science, facilitated our recognition that the analyst is a full participant, together with the patient, in the coconstruction of an analytic relationship. Second, understanding that development and the psychoanalytic situation occur within and are shaped by intersubjective or relational fields (Atwood and Stolorow, 1984; Mitchell, 1988) left us, as analysts, being far more "real" as affective participants in the analytic encounter.

Drawing on those psychoanalysts who emphasized the pivotal importance of the relationship in psychoanalysis, we are currently amplifying relational communicative processes. Rather than anonymity, we emphasize the analyst's authenticity as central for analytic engagement (Levenson, 1983; Mitchell, 1993; Fosshage, 1994; Aron, 1996; Hoffman, 1998; Frank, 1999, to mention a few). Rather than a blank screen, Renik (1998) stresses "getting real" and Levenkron (in press) speaks of "affective honesty." For Ehrenberg (1992), change occurs at the "intimate edge" of the encounter.

Slavin and Kriegman (1998) believe that the analyst must be impacted and change in response to a patient. That is, the analyst is impacted both by "the needed relationships and the repeated relationships" (S. Stern, 1994). Analysts are inevitably drawn into repetitive interactions with patients (Hoffman, 1983, 1996; Mitchell, 1988; Stern, 1997; Bromberg, 1998), and through their personal availability cocreate new relational experiences (Kohut, 1977; Stolorow, Brandchaft, and Atwood, 1987; Fosshage, 1994; Lichtenberg, Lachmann, and Fosshage, 1996; Frank, 1999). Bacal (1985, 1998) speaks of "optimal responsiveness" and "the specificity of selfobject experience in therapeutic relatedness." The self psychology literature is replete with what Lazar (1998) calls "necessary facilitating enactments" (Kohut, 1984; Fosshage, 1995b; Bacal, 1998; Shane, Shane, and Gales, 1997). Hoffman (1996) and Renik (1998) both propose that the spontaneous, authentic moments when the analyst breaks out of the confines of the technical, analytic ritual, are the key moments that bring about change. We (Lichtenberg, Lachmann, and Fosshage, 1996) have written about the effectiveness of disciplined spontaneous engagements, that is, affective enactments of spontaneous communication by the analyst that emerge (erupt) within the structure of an analytic relationship. Benjamin (1990) speaks of the importance of mutual recognition to further intersubjective development. Recognizing that anything we do reveals something about us, we now struggle consciously about what to self-disclose in an effort to facilitate development (Hoffman, 1983; Ehrenberg, 1992; Fosshage, 1997; Renik, 1998; Frank, 1999). We may choose, for example, to disclose love for a patient (Shane, Shane and Gales, 1997; Fosshage, 1999) or "erotic countertransference" feelings (Davies, 1994) to further analytic engagement. To round out the comprehensiveness of the analyst's involvement and communications, psychoanalysts are reassessing the meanings and communicative value of physical touch within the analytic encounter (Ruderman, Shane, and Shane, 2000).

Not only have we recognized that an analyst communicates, unconsciously and consciously, in a myriad of ways, subtle and not so subtle, but we have learned that, when guided by a spirit of inquiry, we can broaden the range of verbal and nonverbal communications that we can choose from to effect change. Because the analytic relationship is a human relationship, we have learned that communication of personal elements, of emotionally attuned and responsive aspects of the analyst's experience, can make an intervention effective (Kohut, 1984; Orange, 1995; Aron, 1996; Stern et al., 1998). To be in touch with our affective experience and to utilize it when communicating (listening and responding) with patients is central in effectuating change.

While we are listening and experiencing, we consciously and unconsciously respond, communicating to a patient nonverbally through subtle but noticeable changes in our eyes, face, body tonality, and body movements. When we communicate verbally, we reveal on a moment to moment basis how we are affectively involved with the patient. All of our verbal communications, including exploratory and interpretive communications, contain intonations, metamessages (Wachtel, 1993), bodily and facial expressions, and possible underlying attitudes of warmth or aloofness, of authoritarianism or collaboration, of acceptance or judgment, all of which contribute to the patient's implicit and explicit relational experience of the analyst. The music of our language (Knoblauch, 2000) as well as the content communicate our meanings.

The creation of an atmosphere of interest, friendliness, and safety is central for facilitating communication (Lichtenberg,

Lachmann and Fosshage, 1996). What are the tonal qualities and metamessages of our outgoing telephone message? Is it welcoming? Is it warm, yet professional? Is it cool and unapproachable? How do we greet the patient in the waiting room for the first and subsequent sessions? From our current understanding that we are always revealing ourselves to the patient, we feel that an analyst's warmth, friendliness, and personal openness contributes substantially to the creation of a facilitating environment (Lichtenberg, Lachmann, and Fosshage, 1996). While we easily recognize that these qualities of communications are facilitative in personal relationships, the emphasis on the blank screen, anonymity, and neutrality has precluded their recognition within the psychoanalytic arena.

We give an illustration of poignant affective communications that emerged out of sustained mutual participation, cocreating "moments of meeting."

I (JLF) had been seeing a 30-year-old man for almost two years. He had sought treatment because of work and relationship problems. He was not sure that he was cut out to be in his profession, had difficulties concentrating, and clearly was not thriving in his work. Currently Max had major problems with his girlfriend of two years, "who was the only person in his life who knew him and cared about him."

For most of his life Max reported that he had underachieved and had experienced a periodically intensifying chronic depression. He had used drugs earlier in his life and continued to gamble in order to stimulate himself. His father, who had died five years earlier, was a physician and, while Max was able to idealize him to some extent, he experienced his father as involved in his work and unavailable. His mother still worked in an academic setting. Max experienced her as "weird," into her own world, and unrelated. She hoarded newspapers and magazines in boxes that took over much of her home. Even though both parents were well educated, neither parent took interest in Max's choice of college. In fact, they did not know his choice until just prior to his departure.

Because of his depression and underachieving, Max had tried psychotherapy and psychoanalysis four times, to no avail. He felt unconnected to all the therapists except the last, whom he had liked. Nevertheless, the last therapy had not helped either, and after a year and a half he left treatment. Six months later, Max's father died and Max called back to see his last analyst. He felt deeply rejected when he experienced his former analyst as "curt" and saying that he did not have time to see him. Although not currently on medication, several prior antidepressants had proved to be ineffective. He was willing to try psychoanalysis one more time because of the pressing problems in his relationship to his girlfriend and his unhappiness at work.

Although he wanted to be helped, based on a lifetime experience of emotional neglect, Max entered treatment half-heartedly. He did muster up some hope, but with considerable skepticism with regard to its potential efficacy. With such very limited expectations, he was difficult to engage. Our joint exploration and inquiry typically lacked affect. Even on those occasions when I felt touched by his plight and spoke more emotionally, Max in his skepticism remained untouched. I took some hope in the fact that Max had remained in treatment for a record time, suggesting that we were forging a relationship.

During one session, Max was troubled by an incident at work. Max tended to feel like a victim (as in his family), assuming no participatory role. Responding to his flatness and repetitiveness of this pattern, I decided to pursue the incident more vigorously. I attempted to explore the incident in detail from a number of angles, looking for traction to understand his interaction with his boss. Max adroitly averted each exploratory thrust. I thought briefly about highlighting our interaction, attempting to raise it to a level of reflection, but felt convinced that it would fall "flat," lacking in affect and reflection. I experienced frustration and a sense of disbelief that he could avert exploration so facilely at every turn (data emanating from what I [Fosshage, 1995a, 1997] have called the other-centered listening/experiencing perspective). In an attempt to reach him affectively and out of my frustration, I "chose" to address it in a clearly exaggerated, yet serious manner and said, "You're pissing me off. Every time I attempt to explore this incident you fend me off." Max was a bit stunned and "wide-eyed." We then proceeded to discuss the interactions with, from my perspective, more affective engagement.

The following session Max returned and immediately said, "You know that is the most emotional that I have ever experienced you." I questioned, "You mean when I told you I was pissed off at you?" Max replied, "Yes," and said no more. I inquired, "How did you feel about that?" Max shrugged his shoulders as if it were not a big deal, once again averting further engagement. I knew that to leave Max in silence was not only unhelpful, but it replicated for him the traumatogenic experience of disengagement and not caring. Thus, after a half minute of silence, I spoke, "Have you ever experienced me as emotional previously?" Max replied, "No." I then replied with emotion, "You know there have been other times when I have felt emotional. At times I have felt deeply moved by your plight and caring about you and I believe that I have expressed it, but I don't think that that registers on your radar screen." Max facially clearly communicated that he was emotionally surprised and touched. This felt like a momentary breakthrough, a moment of meeting, following an emotional sequence between the analytic participants—Max's flat, victimized presentation of a work incident; my inquiry; Max's aversiveness; my exaggerated yet serious expression of frustration and anger; Max's noting my emotional engagement; my more direct expression of caring; and my noting Max's contribution (emotional expressions of caring not registering on his radar screen). At that moment Max and I felt emotionally connected, an antidote to Max's predominate feeling of disconnection.

Forms of Relatedness

We place primary emphasis on helping the patient contact affective experience, needs and intentions (motivations), and related cognition (including thoughts, images, and fantasies). These aspects of lived experience serve developmentally throughout the life span as a wellspring for consciousness and sense of self. Through communicating with herself and with her analyst a patient becomes better acquainted with what she feels, desires, and thinks, contributing to further development of a sense of self.

During analysis, the emergence of different attachment needs and forms of relatedness require different responses, affecting the communicative exchange (Fosshage, 1997, 1999). We conceptualize a range of attachment needs and forms of relatedness. Based on their research, attachment theorists (e.g., Main, 2000) have focused on the need for a sense of safety from the close attachment to a caregiver who is experienced as providing a secure base. These needs are fundamental and come to the foreground particularly during times of experienced danger, abandonment, and loss. Emanating from infant research and dyadic systems theory, mutual regulation of affect is viewed as central (Stern, 1985; Stolorow and Atwood, 1992; Beebe and Lachmann, 1994). Winnicott's "holding" (see Slochower, 1996), Bion's (1962) "containing," and Kohut's (1971, 1984) "omnipotent merger" are all alluding to the mother's role in regulating affect in her infant and, correspondingly, within the analytic relationship (Teicholz, 1999).

In the development of the self, Kohut (1971, 1984) has described "selfobject" needs for acknowledgment and affirmation (mirroring), for an admired, protective other (idealizing), and for a sense of essential alikeness (twinship). These selfobject needs (what Stern, 1985, calls the self-regulating other and Shane, Shane, and Gales, 1997, term the self-transforming other), and corresponding form of relatedness involve the use of another person for development and regulation of a sense of self. Selfobject needs come to the foreground especially during times of self-expansion, stress, and vulnerability.

Another kind of attachment experience involves the need to experience the other's subjectivity in relationship to one's own, a mutual recognition of one another, a dialog between two persons. Stern (1985) and Benjamin (1988, 1995) have called these needs for or connections of self-with-other "intersubjective relatedness"—what Shane, Shane, and Gales (1997) refer to as self with interpersonal-sharing other, and what Jacobs (1998) has aptly termed subject to subject relating. Emde (1988) describes intersubjective relatedness as "I care to know and feel all about us, about you, about me, and about our 'we-ness.'" At these moments a patient desires to encounter more fully the analyst's subjectivity. The analyst must disclose in a broader, less circumscribed manner his subjectivity that enables patient and analyst to recognize one another, the sameness and difference—a form of relatedness emphasized by Benjamin (1990, 1995), Aron (1996), Renik (1998), and others, particularly from the relational perspective.

Another attachment experience involves the need to focus on or be concerned about an other, what we call a "caretaking" relatedness (Fosshage, 1997). Examples are a parent's focusing on and taking care of a child, a teacher of a student, an analyst of a patient. This form of relatedness is highlighted in Erikson's (1959) stage of generativity.

Identifying the attachment need and form of relatedness in the forefront on a moment to moment basis within the psycho-analytic hour substantially impacts effective communicative exchanges. When safety, regulation of affect, and selfobject needs are in the foreground, the analyst's subjectivity is important to the extent that it can be used for developmental and self-regulatory purposes. Other aspects of the analyst's subjectivity can be experienced as intrusive and rupturing of the needed safety and selfobject connection. In contrast, when intersubjective relatedness or self-with-other needs are in the forefront, the insufficient presence of the analyst and the analyst's subjectivity can be experienced as frustrating and as thwarting the developmentally needed connection. One patient, for example, exclaimed, "I need to know your reactions to me as a person, how you experience me in a relationship." And when a patient expresses concern for the analyst, the analyst is faced with a question: is the patient's concern a genuine gesture of "caretaking?" Does it call for graceful acceptance?

The following clinical vignette illustrates the interweaving of selfobject and intersubjective relatedness and the analyst's use of listening/experiencing perspectives (Fosshage, 1995a, 1997) to enhance understanding to facilitate an effective communicative exchange. Several years ago I (JLF) had begun psychoanalytic treatment with a woman, Janice, who was quite labile in mood and prone to fragile self-states. Easily feeling impinged upon, Janice experienced natural light in my office as painfully too bright, for which, at her request, I regularly adjusted the blinds. Both of her parents had been remarkably absent. She described her mother as often feeling overwhelmed. Janice had a prolonged incestuous relationship with her older brother and, when she would cry out to her mother for protection, her mother pushed her away with "leave me alone, you're killing me." She felt that her previous analyst had saved her life and was her first real caretaker. Unfortunately, his move to another city interrupted treatment and forced her to find another analyst, a very painful process.

During a session toward the end of the first month I experienced my consulting room as uncomfortably warm and went to the window to adjust the ventilation. At the following session Janice related how upset she was with me for getting up in the middle of the session, when she was talking, to stare out the window. I was taken aback by what seemed to be a very idiosyncratic perception. Knowing that our capacity to share humor often helped her to regain perspective, I said in a somewhat humorous self-mocking vein, "The mark of a good analyst—get up in the middle of a session and stare out the window." In this instance, it was a misjudgment, for she was far too hurt with her particular experience of the event to join in. Instead, she felt invalidated, and even ridiculed. I then inquired about her experience when I had gone to the window. Janice had felt that I was uninterested in what she was saying. I reflected that her feeling that I went to stare out the window while she was talking and was uninterested in her understandably was quite hurtful to her. She appeared to feel better in that I had heard, understood, and validated her experience. Yet, she was still consumed by the injury and her particular organization of the event. I felt that she needed to free herself from her particular construction of the event in order to regain more fully her self-equilibrium. To that end, I inquired toward the end of the session if she would like to hear about my experience as to what prompted my going to the window. I thought that the discrepancy of our experiences would be useful in illuminating her view of the uninterested other. I hoped to offer her an alternative perspective. She declined.

The following session two days later, Janice told me that she had not wanted to hear my point of view at the previous session and somewhat humorously, yet pointedly, remarked, "Jim, when I come into the room, just check your subjectivity at the door." I smiled and told her that I would try my best, although it could prove difficult on occasion. We then proceeded with her experience and were able to focus on how precarious she felt my interest in her was. It dawned on me what was occurring when she felt overwhelmed by my subjectivity. I interpreted in a gentle manner, "I think I understand that when I do something suddenly, like go to the window, or bring my subjective viewpoint in here, it feels like I am taking up all the space in here, then there is no room for you, for your thoughts and desires." I added, "I sense that you must have felt just that way with your brother." Janice notably relaxed and acknowledged that she thought I was right. Shortly afterward, she smiled and said, "Now, you can let me know what was happening for you at the window."

In light of the rupture and her fragile self-state, Janice needed her analyst to hear and understand that her feelings—selfobject relatedness was in the forefront. It was also crucially important to make sense out of her experience by illuminating the particular relational scenario or organizing pattern that had been triggered—an aspect of self-with-other relatedness—for her to feel understood and to enable her to restore a more positive self-with-other percept. So long as Janice framed the events as indicative of my uninterest in her, she surely would be unable to feel fully restored. My interpretation of the transference was based on two listening/experiencing stances, that is, on my empathic grasp of her experience with me (from within her perspective) and on my other-centered experience as the intrusive, overwhelming other in relationship with the patient (Fosshage, 1995a, 1997). Following the interpretation, Janice felt sufficiently self-consolidated to be able to relate more fully with another (intersubjective relatedness) and inquired about my experience. Subsequent airing of the discrepancies in our experiences further illuminated her particular organization and served as a basis for establishment of an alternative perspective.

Physical Touch as a Form of Communication

Beginning with Freud and Ferenczi, psychoanalysts have wrestled with the issue of physical touch as a form of communication in psychoanalysis. Ferenczi (1953) felt that nurturing touch could facilitate the analysis by helping a patient to tolerate pain that was characterologically defended against. Freud felt that physical contact would almost certainly lead to sexual enactments (see Mintz, 1969b, and Lichtenberg, 1994, for a description of the historical, as well as dynamic, considerations). Freud's rule of abstinence and interdiction on touch has predominated in the psychoanalytic literature. In a few notable exceptions, physical touch is seen not only as appropriate, but as necessary when dealing with periods of deep regression (Balint, 1952, 1968; Winnicott, 1958, 1965) and with psychotic anxieties and delusional transference (Little, 1966, 1990). Bacal (1985) describes how Kohut offered "two fingers" to a deeply depressed patient to hold. Mintz (1969a, 1969b) describes the work of Fromm-Reichman and Searles with deeply disturbed patients. More recently, additional reports of the facilitative use of touch with patients in psychoanalysis have emerged in our literature (Bacal, 1985, 1997; Pedder, 1986; McLaughlin, 1995, 2000; Breckenridge, 2000; Fosshage, 2000; Holder, 2000; Pizer, 2000; Ruderman, 2000; Schlesinger and Appelbaum, 2000; Shane, Shane, and Gales, 2000). Psychoanalysts of different persuasions, in private (Hamilton, 1996), comment that physical contact in the form of handshakes, hand-holding, hugs, and a pat on the back occur with analysands and are usually experienced by both analysand and analyst as facilitative communications. The emergence of psychoanalytic alternatives to classical theory, including more detailed and comprehensive motivational models (the addition of sensuality to sexuality as a motivational system is particularly relevant, Lichtenberg, 1989), and a vast array of empirical studies on the neurobiological functions and psychological meanings of physical touch is helping us to readdress the meanings and communicative use of touch within psychoanalysis.

While physical touch is a fundamental form of communication, to use touch within the psychoanalytic situation can create dangers of "the slippery slope" (Gutheil and Gabbard, 1993; Gabbard, 1994). An analyst's vulnerability, boredom, sensual and sexual deprivation, erotic addiction, self deflation, and professional disillusionment are all psychological issues that can undermine the analytic spirit of inquiry and potentiate a sexual enactment. Nevertheless, in an analysis guided by a spirit of inquiry, touch as one form of broadened communication can occur safely as a disciplined, sometimes spontaneous form of meaningful expression. We briefly describe some of the psychotherapy research findings on touch (see Fosshage, 2000, for a detailed presentation). We then address the use of touch within the psychoanalytic arena, providing several clinical illustrations.

Touch and Clinical Work

Temperament and lived experience affect a person's desire for and comfort level with touch, and the use of touch for communication. People differ as to sensuality and, what is commonly known, as "the gift of touch." The meanings and use (or not) of touch in the analytic dyad emerge out of a complex interaction of two participants and their respective subjectivities. Certain kinds of touch, "giving" as well as "receiving," can be facilitative of therapeutic "moments" and analytic work. For some dyads, touch can be at times traumatizing. A patient's (and an analyst's) desires for touch can be generated out of anxiety, in which case the more important task is to inquire and understand the origins of the anxiety.

An analyst's comfort or discomfort with an analysand's request for hand shaking, hand holding, or a hug is revealing of the patient, the analyst, and the interaction. Occurring within a dyad, the analyst must feel comfortable and authentic in order to create a facilitative interaction involving touch. The mix of genders and ages within the dyad undoubtedly affects meanings and comfort levels for both parties. On those occasions when we, as analysts, feel uncomfortable and recognize that the discomfort is primarily "ours," openly acknowledging our discomfort (maintaining authentic engagement), rather than pathologizing the patient's desire for physical contact (e.g., "acting in"), will facilitate the analytic interaction.

Psychotherapy research and clinical experience make clear that touch, as with all interventions, must be in keeping with the desires and needs of the patient and with the level of intimacy in the relationship (Gelb, 1982; Horton et al., 1995). Touch, as initiated by analyst or patient, can have very different (positive or negative) meanings for each member of the dyad. Physical contact can create a sensual experience or stir sexual feelings (Lichtenberg, 1989; Lichtenberg, Lachmann, and Fosshage, 1992, 1996), as can a look, intonation, and verbal remark. When sexual feelings are stirred within the analytic encounter, they, like all feelings, need to be accepted, understood, and modulated. A large study found that sexual attraction did not interfere with touch being experienced as positive (Horton et al., 1995), suggesting that sexual feelings can be appropriately modulated when touch is used as a form of communication. Occurrences of touch, like all interactions, need to be closely tracked and often discussed for understanding their meanings and for assessing whether they are facilitating or encumbering the therapeutic endeavor.

We have found that touch less often occurs during sessions, perhaps because of the focus on and potential of interfering with an analysand's articulation of experience. When trauma is activated in the analysis, however, touch may be required for reestablishing an empathic connection. During sessions with periods of intense depersonalization and disorientation, touch, combined with simultaneous articulation of experience, can be used to foster a sufficient sense of protection and safety for the reintegration of dissociated memories and affect.

Our first clinical vignette involves the treatment of an adolescent girl who was emotionally frozen. As treatment proceeded, she began to feel again. During one hour, the patient cried and described deep feelings of sadness about her family. At the end of the session, I (JDL) stopped it as gently as I could, but realized that it was disruptive to the patient. On the way out, the patient, having been raised in Europe, automatically reached out to shake my hand. I reached out to meet her hand and then spon-

taneously placed my left hand on top of her right hand, enclos-
ing it. We looked into each other's eyes, each understanding that
I was offering comfort and solace in the face of her sadness and
the disruption. At that moment, physical action (that is, touch
and eye expression) was in the foreground; inquiry was in the
background and served as a basis of internally informing the analyst, providing a stabilizing gyroscopic-like function during the
interaction.

With another patient, during an intense period of traumatic
disruption, holding hands for a few moments during sessions
became a powerful avenue of reconnecting. This occurred in the
analysis of Susan, described earlier. A mirroring bond gradually
intensified through a combination of empathic understanding
and my (JLF) more direct communication of affirming feelings
to her through my words, vocal tonality, facial expressions, and
physical touch. Touch involved on occasion a brief placement of
my hand on her shoulder as she was walking out the door, a playful light kicking of her shoe during the session, and, later, a hug
at the door as she was leaving the session. For Susan, physical
touch was a particularly powerful and meaningful form of communication, for it was through touch that she had most poignantly
connected with her father (sitting on his lap and cuddling) and
non-English speaking grandmother (hugs). Susan, in addition,
was temperamentally a very sensual woman for whom touch was
an important form of communication. The moments of physical
contact with her father and grandmother were the singular
moments in her childhood when she had felt loved and valued.

Because of my particular background and temperament, I feel
relatively comfortable with the use of touch to communicate.
Within the intersubjective context of Susan and myself, I came
upon a light, playful kick of Susan's shoe (sitting face to face) at
certain times when making an interpretation that I thought she
might experience as humiliating. The playful kick, expressing a
reassuring affection, usually elicited a warm smile, and helped her
to sustain reflective capacity.

The traumatic negative percepts of her self and of her analyst
as insufficiently valuing her were easily triggered. Susan and I

were well acquainted with these themes and their origins. On those occasions when a combination of my actions and Susan's constructions triggered her traumatic states, her negative percepts, marked with shame, humiliation and deflation, took over and her reflective capacity vanished. Her body began to shrink, her eyes partially closed, and her gaze dropped to the floor, rarely risking a glance at me for fear of what she might find. At one point, Susan, like the hesitant little girl at the doorway watching her father read his newspaper, hesitantly asked if she could hold my hand. Experiencing her taking a scary risk to reconnect, I responded in the affirmative, moved my chair forward, and reached out to her. Susan and I held both hands, face to face. We sat in silence, feeling the connection. I felt warmth, caring, and affection toward her. She hesitantly dared to look at me, quickly turned away, and then returned again for a longer look. Slowly we described what was happening. Hand holding powerfully communicated that I cared for and valued her, an experience she sorely needed. She gradually was able to reemerge from her traumatic state and to regain reflective capacity and a different, far more benign, perspective on what had occurred. Subsequently, when Susan was in the throes of these traumatic states, hand-holding on occasion added the necessary ingredients of affection and reassurance for breaking through. My experience, as I told her, was that holding hands on these particular occasions had felt to me like a direct avenue to her heart, to her feeling valued again. And, of course, I was feeling deeply that way toward her. In these traumatic states Susan often struggled with negative body images and feelings of repulsion. Holding her hands implicitly conveyed my sense of her physical "touchability" and her physical attractiveness (Kohut's gleam in the mother's eye) that helped her to emerge from her negative percepts and to reinstate her more vitalizing feelings of attractiveness once again. Would words have sufficed? Although we can never know for sure, in this instance I felt that touch, because of its particular meaning for this analysand, was needed to communicate at a fundamental level to break through the traumatic states and co-create the needed reassuring (holding) experience. Would touch have sufficed? Again we cannot know for sure, but I believe our discussions placing our interactions in the context of her need and my openness to respond added immeasurably to our cocreated experience and her growing self-awareness.

Touch is a form of communication that can be integrated into the spirit of inquiry in facilitating understanding and communication in the analytic encounter. As we expand our view of the possible meanings of touch beyond the pejorative (for example, an infantile wish or "acting in"), we can better understand our analysands' requests for or spontaneous gestures involving touch. It can afford analysts greater comfort with physical touch and, regardless of whether an analyst chooses to touch or not, he or she will be better able to work flexibly and constructively with its various meanings.

Concluding Remarks

In this chapter, we have focused on additional inroads for understanding and effecting change within the psychoanalytic encounter. Drawing on developmental, cognitive, psychotherapy, and neuroscientific research, as well as on psychoanalytic theory and clinical experience, we have focused on implicit/nondeclarative and explicit/declarative domains, intractability of mental models, the analyst's affective participation, forms of relatedness, and physical touch as a form of communication.

In our view, *the spirit of inquiry* serves as the foundation of the psychoanalytic process. The analyst usually takes the lead in supplying the initial commitment to the spirit of inquiry, although patients vary as to their natural bent toward and development of reflective capacity. Gradually the patient joins what becomes a shared spirit of inquiry. Once this happens analyst and patient strive to explore, understand, and communicate, creating a "spirit" of interaction that contributes, through gradual incremental learning, to new implicit relational knowledge.

This spirit, as part of the implicit relational interaction, is a cornerstone of the analytic relationship and a crucial component of vital human relationships. The "inquiry" more directly brings explicit/declarative processing to the foreground in the joint attempt to explore and understand. The spirit of inquiry in the psychoanalytic arena highlights both the autobiographical scenarios of the explicit memory system and the mental models of the implicit memory system as each contributes to a sense of self, other, and self with other. This process facilitates the extrication and suspension of the old models, so that new models based on current relational experience can be gradually integrated into both memory systems for lasting change.

CHAPTER FIVE

TRANSFERENCE AS COMMUNICATION: THE LANGUAGE OF THE BODY

How does the past speak? From the time Freud recognized the significance of the past, analysts have tried to find increasingly effective ways to reveal the secrets of prior experience, namely, the archeological metaphor. Memory provided an obvious starting point. Problems of what does or doesn't get recorded, what is then distorted, forgotten, or revised makes memory an unreliable source. Then came a great discovery. Unbeknown to Freud's patients, they began to react to him not as their doctor but as if he were a specific figure from their past. Freud called this transference. This remarkably astute clinical observation was couched in terms of energic cathexes—a theoretical construct that limited recognition of the power of this form of communication in the organization of all daily life. From a contemporary standpoint, we may say that the image transferred was not that of a real or distorted picture of a person but a map of a relationship with affective motivational implications. The current way of experiencing was not a camera-like projection of a past experience in static and real time form—a virtual image—but more of a shadow cast over and enmeshed with current experiences. We believe that the outline of the past recognized under the rubric of transference can be given its full significance by seeing the process through the broadened context provided by our way of viewing communication.

First, to simplify: transference is a way to describe conscious and especially unconscious expectations people have that guide the manner in which they construe (give meaning to) their current experience. How are such expectations formed? As we described in chapter 1, repetitive, lived experiences lead to an event map becoming categorized and generalized. Mapping involves more than an experiential scene. Cognitive processing creates inferences that involve self, others, motivation, affect, and causality—no matter how primitive. A child whose experiences are that she has been treated fondly and sensitively will infer a number of interrelated, largely unconscious beliefs, one about others, one about herself, and one about alternatives. She will believe about others that they are likely to respond to her with fondness and sensitivity. She will believe that she is a person who can elicit fondness and sensitivity and that she is worthy of such responses—a loveable child. She will believe that discrepant experiences exist (and have been categorized) so that in some contexts she can expect to be treated without fondness and sensitivity. Stated simply, every expectation contains a dominant pattern and a pattern of exceptions. The coexistence of a dominant expectation and an exception is particularly important for children and adults whose lived experience has been troubling or traumatic. Their dominant expectation leaves them hypervigilant to perceptions that confirm "Oh my, here it's happening again." The coexisting alternative: "This time it can and will be different" provides the hope that leads them to seek, utilize, and sustain therapy. Expectations and the inferences drawn from them antedate the symbolic coding that is subsequently used to describe them. Language has the remarkable capacity successfully to delineate positive and negative expectations and inferences about oneself and others. This very fact may indicate that expectations and inferences that are the bedrock of infant experience may have provided constraints that guided the very formation of language.

Now to add the needed complexity—lived experiences in infancy are extremely varied, flowing with easy or jarring transitions from one to another. Accordingly, expectations will be multiple or even could be infinite. We have described contexts that help to give organization to shifting lived experiences and therefore to broad categories of expectations. During those moments during which physiological needs are ascendent and being responded to more or less effectively, a contextually influenced set of expectations about self, about other, and about alternative possibilities are formed. Similarly, the context of moments during which attachment needs for intimacy on the part of infant, caregiver or both are ascendent will lead to another set of expectations of self and other, along with discrepant possibilities. Moments of sensual-sexual arousal, and of aversively dominated experience establish contexts with different expectations. All these other contexts of physiological requirements, attachment, aversiveness, and sensuality provide different expectations from the moments in which exploration is dominant. Each of these contexts can be delineated when a particular need is clearly ascendent providing support for the categorization of five motivational systems. Alternatively, for many, many moments, one need and associated context blends into another, exploring being an easily recognized aspect of a child at play with toys but also when looking over a stranger, trying out a new taste, or testing how demanding and oppositional he can be with a new baby sitter.

Each expectation is both context-sensitive and an active component in further elaborating that context. A 10-year-old desperately needs help with math. His expectation (possibly unformulated) is that his teacher rather than help will shame him—"Why can't you listen in class?" We can easily picture the awkward, hesitant, defensive manner of his approach to his teacher, which, in turn, influences the response he is apt to get. Further, his antenna will be constantly monitoring the cues. Is the message he is sensing (accurately or not) that he is an unwelcome nuisance? He may infer unconsciously the confirmation of his negative expectation from the slightest of cues, such as a momentary glancing away by the teacher or even a telephone call coming as he approached. When the negative expectation is very strong from past lived experiences and has been reconfirmed by recent events and interactions, unconscious searching for a disconfirming response may require cues that are unambiguous and strongly positive.

If transference is regarded as expectations based on inferences drawn from lived experiences and organized in contexts formed in conjunction with shifting motivational systems, then what aspect of an individual's daily life isn't transference? By this definition, some aspects of expectations are always changing, but the phenomenon of casting a shadow from the past on the present is unending. Inevitably, through their role in the categorizing and recategorizing of each new experience, largely unformulated expectations not only share the current experience but also create a new future and a reshaping of the past.

If conscious and unconscious expectations are ubiquitous factors influencing all experience, what distinguishes transference as a form of communication within psychoanalysis? Psychoanalysis provides a context that, by virtue of the spirit of inquiry, allows us to unwrap the overall packaging in which the expectations of two people influence their ongoing communicative exchanges. The unfolding of expectations has been most commonly recognized in direct verbal and nonverbal foreground exchanges. The content of these communications may be and often is similar to what an analysand may tell his best friend, spouse, or barber. But these socially adept listeners are less likely to display the same receptivity to identify systematically the teller's experience from the teller's point of view, and then to search for contexts and meanings to be reflected back. The many times during analysis when an analyst systematically (but not exclusively) suspends his point of view and self-interest in the interest of apprehending the patient's state of mind constructs a unique frame of exploration. In exchanges during which an empathic mode of perception is dominant, the patient's communications to the analyst are folded back to the patient through the analyst's understanding. The analyst's communications provide the patient with an experience of being mirrored in his feelings, thoughts, and intuitions, or of having his inner world shared, or of being cared for, by a person worthy of deep respect, such eventualities in themselves enhancing to the patient. All of this occurs in the foreground when the patient communicates feelings, wishes, and values formulated verbally and nonverbally in a fashion that the analyst becomes able to perceive empathically.

However, frequently expectations are poorly formulated, especially when expressive of relived traumatic disruptions, or of amorphous enmeshment in pathological accommodations, or of fiercely aversive, repetitive and inflexibly concretized beliefs. The channels for expression of these heavily burdened expectations are varied. When enacted in the treatment setting they pull the analyst off his listening stance into role-dominated responses. Now the analyst must be open to some level of participation in the engagement and turn his listening to the particular form of "otherness" he plays out in his role within the enactment.

When the channel for expression is a full-blown affect state such as rage, depression, euphoria, panic, or shame-humiliation, the analyst must address the impact of the patient's emotion, knowing that the patient's own capacity for cognition, exploration, or reflective awareness is severely compromised. He must help in the containment of the more impinging affects and assist the patient's restoration of attachment after periods of dissociation and withdrawal.

When the channel for expression is through body symptoms and sensations as in the case of Harry that we will present, the inaccessibility of affect recognition and other linkage to triggering events puts the analyst in the position of having to find means to communicate with words about the unverbalized experience. All of these situations of heavily burdened expectations have in common patients' belief that their pain will not be appreciated and their cry not heard. Thus before exploration can be effective, moments of analysts communicating as external observers, even protecting their self-interest, will be mixed with moments in which empathic perception can prevail. In her theory of the multiple coding of affective experience, Bucci (1997) identifies a nonverbal subsymbolic mode of encoding emotional experience that includes sensory, somatic, and motoric components. This mode coexists with a nonverbal symbolic imagic mode and a symbolic verbal mode. Trauma leads to pathological dissociation between the modes. Treatment works to build connections among the dissociated experiences, leading in time to their integration. We believe that in problematic situations in which long periods of blurred, confusing, dissociated communication prevent more focused exploration, the analyst's dedication to a spirit of inquiry is essential to sustain an analytic process.

Experientially, analyses, like all significant relationships, are anchored by a background sense of safety. In analysis the background of safety is created to a large extent by the analyst. The sense of safety is contributed to by the analyst's empathic listening, her sensitivity to the nuances of conversational exchanges, and her openness to approach all verbal and nonverbal interactions with open-ended curiosity. Especially in those not-infrequent situations in which the patient's corrosive past experiences have led to intensely held expectations of danger, doing, and relating is probably less significant than "being" (Winnicott, 1965). Analysts convey implicit knowledge of their being through the nonverbal, nonlinear communications that flow largely silently into the intersubjective field. We are not speaking here of countertransference but of an essential integrity and honesty that characterizes analysts' inquiry into their own inner world. We see the spirit of inquiry as an essential component of the analyst's contribution to the sense of safety for both partners. Through this aspect of analysts' exploratory attitude, they silently invite the analysand to join them in discovery, novelty, playfulness, and reflection.

Clinical Illustration

Harry was in his late 20s when he began his treatment with me. Movie star handsome and athletically active, he nonetheless conveyed an awkwardness in his body movements. The most immediately striking aspect of his presentation was that he talked continuously, repeating the same comments over and over. If I indicated that I heard what he was saying, he evidenced no change. By the third repetition whatever mild affect had been present in the initial rendering was gone. If I asked him to expand on a theme he nodded and ignored my request. If I commented on his mode of expression he became confused and appeared stoned— a state familiar to him after years of pot and drug use during his entire adolescence. Although he gave no overt evidence or recognition of being anxious, on his leaving, the back of his shirt and the chair were generally wet. He would sometimes say that words I used that to me were gentle left him feeling as if he had been hit on the side of his head with a two-by-four. I have no doubt that he could sense my frustration with the repetition and overall affective aridness of his communication; however, the allusion to the two-by-four on the side of his head referred to a somatic memory of being struck there by his father in a state of fury. I didn't learn about the physical assaults until much later.

Every week or two Harry announced that he had the flu or was coming down with it. At first I thought he was prone to repeated viral episodes. Then I began to wonder if he was using a somatic sensation as a signal of stress. Since he was not prone to make causal links between somatic complaints and life events, I took another tack. In *Beyond Interpretation* (1979) Gedo described this as "teaching" the patient essential psychological approach as a preinterpretive strategy. I inquired in detail about his symptoms and offered him a medical description of the flu including an elevated temperature. Miraculously my directness and sincere interest captured his responsiveness and he concluded that what he had—which we both agreed was something—was not the flu. He had come to call it that because that was what his mother said she had when she took to her bed for days or weeks after hypomanic social arranging or massive intrusions into her children's lives. If Harry told his mother he was unhappy, or worried, or angry, she would chatter on about her own interests, but if he told her he was physically ill, she would become sympathetic and focused. The difficulty for Harry was that mother's solicitude for his physical state activated his father's contempt and anger. A fight would ensue about his staying home from school. What happened between us was that I enacted with Harry a positive focus on his flu sensations without his father's contempt.

In place of the flu, we began to go directly to areas of stress. After attending the best private schools, Harry had barely finished high school due to his drug usage. He had been sent to a therapeutic school which he left to play in a rock band. Harry had no memory of the band, the music they played, or who the other members were; he remembered only the girls they "messed with" and the drugs they took. I knew from things he said that the band had been successful, but Harry persisted in denying any knowledge of or interest in music. Only years later did Harry recall and reconnect with the other members who had gone on to have distinguished careers in music. After the years of drifting, Harry returned home, stopped using drugs, and enrolled in the business school of a fine college. He mentioned that college was taking a long time, and I discovered Harry was taking only a few courses. If he did poorly, he dropped the course. Poorly it turned out was not getting an A. If he took only one course a semester he could memorize even the fine print and so ensure an A. And nothing but an A might get the attention of his father, a Phi Beta Kappa from an Ivy League college. With this information we could connect a host of somatic complaints—headache, upset stomach, nebulous skeletal pains—with worry over courses and exams. However making connections between symptoms and stresses had little ameliorative effect. I began to discuss with him approaches to study, the use of outlines, the way to appreciate significance rather than needing to "know" everything. Harry began to take on a full course load and graduated with honors. Regrettably, his family members were too caught up in their own preoccupations to appreciate his accomplishment.

During sessions, unpredictably, Harry might hide his face in his hands and cry in a flood of sudden sadness. His associations might either be to the death of someone close or to feelings about someone who had been kind to him.

Harry seemed always to be getting injured. His mother told him that when he was a little boy his tall father carried him on his shoulders and failed to notice doorways or ceilings, so Harry frequently hit his head. Harry's parents went on frequent pleasure trips leaving the children with sitters they knew little about.

One sitter punished the children by locking them in the base-ment while another had been sexually seductive. The children engaged in wild and often dangerous play, with Harry at times tak-ing the role of protector and at other times that of a participant.

In home movies taken by his grandfather, Harry, at age five, is seen running back and forth giving toys or food to his younger brother and sister. His parents are off skating, skiing, or sailing. As the camera centers on him, Harry makes awkward wild flut-tering movements with his raised arms and hands. These move-ments are more exaggerated examples of movements he made during sessions when he talked anxiously and self-consciously. The impression was that he was being required to put on a per-formance he is extremely ambivalent about. As a teenager, Harry became an excellent tennis player, but in tournaments, as soon as he felt he was expected to win, his coordination would disin-tegrate into an ineffectual flutter.

Harry's basic expectation was that he was permanently embed-ded in a large family of people each of whose disorganization and dysregulation were equal to or more often greater than his. He would have to look after them with no one listening to, or car-ing about, what he thought or felt. Harry and his next younger brother fought incessantly to the point of battering. When they were teenagers, their father, presumably to stop their fighting, would wade in and batter them both. Harry engaged in various sports but the frequency of his injuries puzzled me. After many injuries, I found out that when his leg or shoulder or back hurt he would continue to play or run for hours, exhausting himself and aggravating the injury. Pain was not a signal for him to stop. Incidentally, his brother's response to physical and psychic pain was compulsively to practice his musical instrument (he is a renowned musician) and to take addictive drugs. Harry consulted doctors regularly about all of his injuries but paid little attention to their advice. After our discovery of his continuing exertions despite pain, he was told to rest his injured right shoulder. I noticed some weeks later that he wasn't moving his right arm. He said he was resting it because of his awareness of the pain when he moved it. I was alarmed by this overresponse in the opposite direction. Harry sought an orthopedic consultation and discovered he had a frozen shoulder requiring weeks of physiotherapy and specialized exercise.

Harry displayed none of the ordinary manifestations of transference. He made no direct attributions, showed no curiosity, raised no issues about fee, and rarely missed a session. He was extremely aversive to change—whether the timing of his hours or anything in his outside life. My function was to be a reliable stabilizer, a counterforce against his disorganization and detachment. Despite the major psychopathology in the family (three of his siblings had been hospitalized at one time or another), the family was close-knit. Whoever had a problem told the mother, who came up with an erratic solution and started a round of calls that agitated each of the members, who then called each other, furthering the agitation. My repeated drawing his attention to this pattern helped him establish some restraint.

After college, Harry had to confront the question of what to do and decided to enter the financial world. To do so, he had to oppose his parents who were both against the acquisition of money. Father was a philanthropist bent on giving away the family fortune and mother had the utmost contempt for everyone but artists. To oppose them, Harry had to see himself as following in the footsteps of early generations who had been highly successful entrepreneurs. He had to see himself in impractical grandiose terms to justify following his own goal. After much discussion, he started at a beginner's level, rapidly demonstrated an entrepreneurial flair, and gradually persuaded his father to let him take over more and more of the family's resources. Here he was activating a familiar pattern. As the oldest, he looked out for his siblings whenever he could. As his mother's confidant, he had to side with her in her persecutory complaints. Now he could also rescue his father from giving away so much money he had no more to give. I could appreciate his skill at investing which allowed him to talk more freely about his intense anxiety about changes in the stock market. If it went up, his clients, like his family, would expect only more and if it went down, he would be held in contempt.

After several years of treatment Harry married Mary, a young woman from a working-class family. He showed little interest in

Mary's work, thoughts, or feelings, complaining to her about his symptoms as he had with his mother. She never complained about his indifference but began to have complaints of her own about her bowels, heart, and lungs that verged on the delusional. Hoping to break through her denial, Harry railed at her to tell him her feelings until finally Harry's father got her to go to an appropriate treatment facility. The behavioral conditioning therapist prescribed that she confine her incessant somatic complaints to one hour per day. During that hour Harry was to write down everything she said without criticism or comment. This reconditioning exercise helped to restore their prior way of living together but did nothing to improve the intimacy of their attachment. Years later after another severe episode of somatic symptomatology following the death of her father, Mary accepted the idea that her symptoms were related to emotional stress and in desperation began treatment.

I believe Harry to be a D-category (disorganized/disoriented) attachment child with a subcategory of anxious-resistant attachment who became an anxious preoccupied adult caregiver for his family. He was raised by a disorganized mother with psychothymic tendencies and proneness to panic episodes that frightened the children and by a father with severe narcissistic pathology and rage responses. Harry became hypersensitive to his mother's affective states, adopting the strategy of becoming her caregiver in a role reversal to assure an insecure attachment. They enacted between them the pattern of taking turns at soliciting caregiving responses from the other through physical illnesses and bodily complaints. This strategy was defective in that it resulted in his father's contempt and failed to elicit consistent responses form his mother. Whatever she praised or sympathized in one moment she would condemn the next. Procedural memories were organized around abuse and fear leading to skeletal awkwardness and vulnerability to pain and to physical expression of anxiety (his sweating). Because of the tendency to emotional detachment and dissociation, event memories were poorly organized and disconnected from the contexts in which they occurred. Metaphorically expressed in somatic sensation, aversive experiences become detached from their emotional origins. For a patient like

Harry, the compelling nature of somatic discomfort, intense autonomic system triggering, and actual physical pain elicit a sense of
reality that talk therapy could dislodge only after a strong foundation of safety had been established. Strong aversive physical
sensations, similarly to affective aversive states, compel an inward
focus that makes it impossible for a person either to decenter and
take another perspective or to use higher-level cognitive reasoning of any sort. The disconfirmation that physicians may offer carries little or no weight against the power of the sensation and its
underlying unconscious conviction that something is seriously awry.

Reflective Awareness and the Role of Verbal Exchanges

Reflective awareness and metacognitive monitoring have traditionally been regarded as intrapsychic developmental functions.
Whether considered as a person's tracking reflectively his or her
own thoughts and feelings or being able to reflect on another
person's thoughts and feelings, these capacities are developmentally and operationally part of an intersubjective field. We recognize that a great deal of many experiences, especially those of
early childhood, remain unformulated (Stern, 1997) and that
much of what is formulated is done so nonlinearly. Daniel Stern
and other members of the Change Process Study Group (Stern
et al., 1998) propose that, as an analytic treatment moves along,
patient and analyst work at an implicit relational level. In the
course of ordinary analytic work, analyst and patient guided by
ordinary technique experience themselves as "moving along."
However, at some point in the treatment patient and analyst are
moved emotionally to meet in an encounter during which the
authenticity of their more spontaneous relatedness transcends
technique. These occurrences, when "the book is thrown away,"
are referred to as "now moments." The language used here—
moving along, meeting in an authentic encounter, spontaneity—
parallels that of movement and dance therapy (Siegel, 1984).
Implicit relational learning during talk and movement therapies
contributes to a background sense of trust and safety as well as

giving form and color to a foreground expectation of hope. Using this formulation, how do repetitive pathological expectations become reorganized? The Stern group's view is that implicit relational procedures that unconsciously governed enactive forms of "being with a person" become destabilized. An open space allows for "creative disorder and internal flux" "during which the deconstructed enactive representation can be co-constructed into more adaptive but equally complex new ways of being together."

This account of therapeutic change is compatible with proposals we have set forward. We have suggested that three processes inherent in ordinary growth are integral to exploratory therapies. These are: (1) self-righting or resilience when an inhibitory stress has been removed; (2) joint or shared expanding awareness parallel to the experience of a mother and her baby expanding their explicit and implicit knowledge of the other and of themselves together; and (3) the reorganization of representational schema. The view of open-space moments of creative disorder during which previously fixed aversive expectations can be coconstructed into an alternative positive expectation is compatible with our view of how representational schema become recategorized. We regard a pivotal cause to be a discrepancy between a negative transferential expectation seeming to be realized in the on-going treatment and the contrasting alternative perception of the analyst as a consistent, reliable, empathic responder. Conversely, a positive (idealizing) transference expectation seeming to be realized in the ongoing treatment may be countered by a contrasting alternative perception of the analyst's inevitable empathic failings, professionally necessary distancing, and billing.

At the end of the movie *Dancing at Lugnasa*, a member of that dysfunctional family states: "Dancing as if language had surrendered to movement. Dancing as if language no longer existed because words were no longer necessary." If the basis for change lies in now-moments, in implicit relational learning, or even in experiences of mirroring, twinship sharing, and idealization, *why talk at all?* If verbalization as with Harry involves so fragmented a narrative and provides so little informative communication, what was to be gained from continuing to talk? The Stern group (1998) state that one effect of working at an implicit relational level is to create increasingly collaborative forms of dialogue. This did happen very gradually with Harry. But a question still remains: What part does exploratory talk play in recovery? Let us shift from the topographic metaphor of open space to a time metaphor. How long does a positive experience such as an attunement link between an infant and mother take? Very little as research has demonstrated. Schore (1994) believes that a negative affect such as shame can occur instantly as a direct right hemisphere to right hemisphere communication. A creative thought—in the form of words, imagery, or sensation—may have a long period of incubation but can occur in a flash in waking moments or in a dream. Alternatively, reflecting, considering, chewing over, tracking back, pausing to let something sink in, giving the other person a chance to join in, all take more time. The argument has been advanced that time-consuming linear reasoning comes after the therapeutic job has been done, an icing on the cake. To paraphrase *Dancing at Lugnasa*, words were no longer necessary; dancing or nonlinear processes had carried the treatment.

Both in principle and from experience, we find it hard to subscribe to a notion that only a part of the brain's capacity is used in the arduous task of restructuring pathological organizing patterns. However, even if we ascribe major leverage to nonlinear elements, we nonetheless can assign critically important functions to verbal linear exchanges: placing in context, highlighting and fixing in memory, opening to alternatives, and providing a scaffolding for reflectiveness in inner speech. Each time patients describe a traumatic event they give themselves an opportunity to put the event into a context to gain a greater perspective on the motives of others and of themselves. Each time patients verbally review their feelings about a loss, they can decenter from their personal pain and place the loss in the all-too-human perspective of life and death. More importantly, each time analyst and patient review the nature of a transference attribution, looking at its origins and adding to their initial prespective the revisions gained from the view of the other, they enrich the conceptual field in which they must operate.

Therapists use linear reasoning to identify patterns like Harry's verbal repetitiveness and to draw inferences about its origins in the rigidly held expectation that he will not be listened to. Then, sharing the observation in words highlights the issue—that is, brings it into awareness and marks it as a pattern having significance. Marking verbally, describing, and labeling help to fix the issue in memory, allowing for a point of reference. The clear verbal expression of an issue for investigation is especially needed with patients prone to somatization, detachment, and dissociation such as Harry.

At a period in analysis when insight and reconstruction were considered central, the release of memory from behind its transference shield was the benefit assumed to be obtained from conflict interpretation. In our view a more important consideration is the patient's openness to ways of thinking, feeling, and acting that differ from possibilities to the unconscious expectations and patterns he or she has been blindly following. However, we believe it is generally the patient's logic that opens the path to an alternative approach rather than the therapist's. When a patient feels that his motives, as they have come to make sense to him, are thoroughly understood and appreciated by the therapist, he can spontaneously enlarge his perspective to consider alternatives previously discarded or never entertained.

Finally, words expressed between therapist and patient will eventually change the way the patient speaks to himself. When a therapist remembers what he and the patient have expressed to each other verbally and nonverbally, like Harry's immobilized shoulder and frightened sweats, a verbal tracking process can begin. Then when the triggering event—a happening or a feeling state or an empathic failure—can be identified, a logical sequence can be constructed. As differing views of the sequence are discussed, moments of reflectiveness, even creative reverie, become possible. These occurrences during sessions provide the scaffolding for patients to build on when alone. They can scan their thoughts and feelings, integrate happenings, and consider alternatives. They can move from self-focused to other-focused and back again. Inevitably this opening to reflectiveness affects both the richness of their inner monologue and the coherence of their narrative in dialogue. "(O)ur capacity to allow our most deeply felt intentions free play in the realm of words . . . leads to conscious choices that are deeply and openly considered. Only the direct engagement with experience that this kind of self-reflection represents gives us the opportunity to lead examined lives" (Stern, 1997, p. 25).

CHAPTER SIX

WORDS, GESTURES, METAPHORS, AND MODEL SCENES

Throughout the early period of psychoanalytic discoveries, words as text were the principal means by which analysts gained the information needed for insight. Images from dreams or gestures needed to be translated into words to appreciate their meaning. The preverbal period of infancy was largely a black box, unrelating and amorphous. With the advent of infant research largely in the last third of the 20th century, the richly textured gestural communicative skills of infants began to be appreciated. As Stern (1985) noted, we are now in a position to ask babies questions and get meaningful answers. Out of these discoveries have come our current appreciation of preverbal and nonverbal communication, of affects as the red thread that runs from infant to adult (Lichtenberg, Lachmann, and Fosshage, 1996), and of implicit relational learning (Stern, et al., 1998). New discoveries excite us, sometimes to the point of imbalance. In chapters 1 and 2 we examined communication in early life as a package—relational, affective, gestural, presymbolic, symbolic—all coming together in a flow that played out in patterns of individuality. Yet something obvious can get lost in the excitement. As clinicians, post-Freudian practitioners of a "talking cure" conducted in a spirit of inquiry, we are still basically dependent on talk, on words, whatever variant of free association we may employ.

Words as Designators

In the early slow process of an infant of about 12 months picking up a word to refer to an "object," observers have assumed that the object—mother, father, or bottle came to be called mama, dada, or ba because the object was of great interest and the labelling word had been used frequently in association with it. In this period the infant's reference point for interest is based on his or her motivation with respect to the "object." A further assumption is that word-learning is greatly enhanced by social cues such as eye gaze, finger pointing, and repetition of naming. As toddlers expand from a predominately solipsistic motivation to a source of intentional focus that includes both their own interest and that of others, the openness to acquiring vocabulary quickens remarkably. The rapid learning of language in this period depends on adults talking about objects, actions, and events that children have already focused on, rather than on a didactic approach. "If the child can 'read' the social situation and if the adult is attuned to the child, then word learning becomes a kind of apprenticeship in which the social environment 'feeds' word-to-world mappings to the child in digestible portions. . . . Children whose parents engage in joint attention such that those parents talk about what those children are looking at tend to have children with advanced vocabularies" (Hollich, Hirsh-Pasek, and Golinkoff, 2000, p. 12). "Children actively seek out information relevant to their interests and adults are happy to provide it" (p. 10). In her discussion of the Hollich et al. (2000) monograph on the origin of word learning, Bloom adds an important caveat in which she integrates motivation with the multiple factors delineated by research. She states that child learners are more than passive perceivers, receivers, or possessors of external supports; rather, the child's intentional state at any particular moment of time and the child's affective appraisals determine whether words are worth learning. "The word learning child is a child with feelings and thoughts about other persons, a child engaged in dynamic real-life events, a child learning to think about a world of changing physical and psychological relationships—in short, a child poised to act, to influence, to gain control, a child reaching out to embrace the learning of language for the power of expression it provides" (Bloom, 2000, p. 133). From the standpoint of motivation systems theory, two motives are active simultaneously. One motive resides in the intention that the adult recognizes and names, as when the infant signals wanting to be picked up and the adult or baby says "up." The second motive comprises the exploratory need/desire to acquire the tools for greater efficacy than having a word to identify an intention provides.

In our view, the intersubjective experience of an analysand and analyst during periods of optimal effectiveness is remarkably similar to that of a toddler during the early stages of rapid language acquisition. When an adult senses what affectively significant intention a child is motivated to focus on and the adult names it and talks about it, a new realm of experience is mapped or, more commonly, an already mapped presymbolic experience is remapped in words. Comparably, when an analyst (or an analysand) senses what affectively significant intention an analysand is motivated to focus on and the analyst (or analysand) names the intention and affect and talks about it, a realm of experience is remapped in a dynamic, verbal, symbolic form. The remapping in verbal form opens the way for exploration of the subjective and intersubjective domain in which the motivation exists. As with the child, these experiences of a motive being recognized, named, and talked about are not dramatic moments of attachment epiphanies or exploratory revelation, so with the analysand they are moments of more subtle explicit and implicit addendums to the knowledge of the dynamics of communication with others and with the self.

An example begins with a supervisor noting to a talented analytic trainee that his patient Clarisse seemed to be telling him that she was ready to recognize her tendency to make astute observations and then avoid drawing the conclusions necessary to alter her patterns of behavior. In their discussion the supervisor used the term "dodging" to describe what Clarisse was doing in the analysis and what the analyst was doing in not recognizing and exploring the pattern. The designator, "dodging," chosen without reflection, connected avoidance as a concept with an evocative physical action familiar to every child.

The analyst waited for his patient's associations to reveal the avoidance pattern as well as indications of the patient's openness to have it designated and recognized. The analyst's "naming" comment to Clarisse occurred toward the end of the last hour of the week. This is the first hour of the subsequent week.

C: I've been thinking more about where we left off with *my dodging things*. . . . And, one way is that *I don't confront things directly. I skirt around the edges.* I was remembering what happened with my father last week. He called me at work and I was terribly busy. I knew I had asked him not to call me during the day. I started to say something but he told me what he always says. He needs my help. His boss is sending him on another trip and he is afraid he's too old and too weak. He's not really, and I know he just wants me to cheer him up and reassure him he can make it.

A: You sound annoyed.

C: Yes, I am. It's hard for me *to figure out what's a dodge and what's not a dodge.*

A: Is that a reaction to what I had said?

C: No, it's a more general question. How could I have responded differently? (Pause) Now I can imagine a *more direct approach* would be to say, "It really frustrates me when you won't listen to me and call me at work and talk on and on."

A: My impression is that your frustration is two-fold: frustration with your father for calling and also feeling responsible to take on his problems and help him. [The analyst is asking the patient to recognize not only what she dodges about her father's intrusiveness but also what she avoids recognizing about a constraint she places on herself—"to be his caregiver."]

C: [Nods yes.]

A: What are you feeling now?

C: I feel annoyed and burdened. . . . Why is my father so needy?' To tell you the truth I know he sucks me into feeling sorry for him when he's no more needy than I am. And what really gets my goat is he'll never acknowledge he calls to lean on me. He says he's just calling to talk. I'd feel better if he could be direct about it and maybe then I could be direct with him.

A: If he made his request in a more direct way would you feel you would have more choice how to respond?

C: Oh, yes. That's what was missing from my childhood. [Pause] I just thought of another thing that happened over the weekend when I was able to be direct with my neighbor Jane. She told me one more episode of how her boyfriend stood her up once again. I knew she wanted me to buy into his excuse about working late and reassure her he loves her. I was able to say, "Do you want to know my opinion?" I think she was startled into saying yes and I told her she had to decide when one more time was one too many. Just accepting his promises and excuses on faith isn't enough. I felt good that I just told her my opinion *directly* and didn't *dance around like* before and *be her comforter.*

A: Again, relieving.

C: Oh, it was. I know it was painful for her to hear, but it was relieving to me and I think maybe to Jane too.

A: You are wondering if maybe she wanted your *straight answers.*

C: Yes, and I tend not to give that.

A: Why do you think that is?

C: I'm just not sure about *straight talk.* Maybe it feels like closing in on someone. Intruding. Being harsh. Hardhearted. You look surprised.

A: More puzzled. [A long pause followed during which Clarisse was unusually silent and thoughtful. During the pause the analyst was riveted by an association to a model scene in which Clarisse against her parents' prohibition had begun smoking and experimenting with drugs. She was frightened about herself and while throwing her butts down the toilet she left her room reeking with the odor of smoke. Her mother never mentioned the odor or asked about Clarisse's smoking. She would leave the window open to clear the smell. Clarisse had described this scene several times and the analyst felt free to refer to it.]

A: Clarisse, have you been smoking? What is going on that you're so upset?

C: [Wells up.]

C: Tears come to my eyes. My mother not asking is so painful. Why couldn't my parents address it directly with me? I needed their help. They would say they didn't want to upset me. They treated me like a baby when I needed to be treated with the respect you only can get when problems get clear.

The sequence of events culminating in the specific interplay of this hour reveals the powerful effect of recognition and naming. The supervisor recognized the patient's aversive motive of avoidance and her (presumed) openness to explore that motive. He recognized that the analyst was enacting a similar pattern of avoiding directly designating the means of avoidance. He also recognized the supervisee's openness to learn from him. The supervisor's intuitive choice of name, "dodging," led the analyst to focus his attention on the process of both his role in the enactment and the patient's associations. In turn, his verbal intervention with the patient led to each having a similar point of focus that they could explore together. All of this bears resemblance to the adult-child experience in naming, learning, and communicating, but with an important difference. Toddlers are absorbing words that label their intentions in order to build increasingly complex maps or nexi of affective symbolized meaning. Adults have the maps or nexi of affective symbolized meaning available and use the naming recognitions during analysis to focus on the maps in order to explore and remap them. The process in analysis has a paradoxical duality. Assigning the word "dodging" to the unrecognized, unacknowledged aversive intention narrows the focus and concentrates the attention of patient and analyst. But then an explosion outwards to the periphery of the existing map takes place with a series of associations to analogous words—"skirting," "dancing around," and to opposites, "confronting," "direct," "getting clear." Incidents and events flood in to provide depth to the exploration, culminating in the analyst's "riveting" association to the model scene or jointly constructed map of the smoke odor. With this shared memory, the patient experiences a liberation of tears of hurt and disappointment at her parents' failure to intervene to protect her.

Disrupted Communication: The Interplay of Gestural and Verbal Modes

In a free-flowing communicative dialogue conducted in a joint spirit of inquiry as in the prior example, words carry the weight of the informational exchange. Naming provides focus and focus opens the way to sharing symbolic meanings and liberating affect. Reflective awareness helps to carry the exploration into new territory. Where intense affective states prevail, however, cognitive acuity is diminished and symbolic meaning is much more difficult to communicate through words. Reflective awareness is lost. For a child in the midst of a tantrum, an adolescent in a drug high, or an adult in a panic, rage, or depressive or dissociative state, words have little explanatory or exploratory power. The affect is the message and from its gestural and impactive dimension a parent or analyst must deduce what the child or patient is conveying and what response will help to prevent further disruption. The child or patient is living in a narrow here and now consciousness, easily made worse and often difficult to make better. An analyst's calmness may be experienced as comforting or as indifference and abandonment. An analyst's active intervention may be experienced as restorative or as provocative and intrusive. Returning to the toddler with the temper tantrum, a mother's verbal directions or explanations will have less restorative value than remaining patiently nearby until the intensity abates; only then will sensitively fondling and soothing facilitate the child's return to a more balanced affective-cognitive state. Nonverbal gestural communication carries the day and leads to intuitive relational learning, but it stops there. For mother and child to open the triggering situation to exploration, words are needed: Mother: "I can't let you play with a sharp knife and I should have given you the play knife daddy bought you. Next time I will, OK?" Child: "OK, next time."

In contrast to the free-flowing verbal exchanges between the prior analysand and analyst, the next example describes the basically nonverbal communication between a depressed, bitter, resistant patient and an analyst trying to foster a minimal attachment experience.

Sonya, a professional woman in her late 20s, was referred by a psychiatrist who was treating another member of her family. Sonya stated in a barely audible voice that she was depressed and had been depressed for as long as she could remember—probably all her life. At the instigation of her mother, she had seen a well-known analyst in another city for a year and it had been no help at all. She stated that most of the time had been spent in silence, as she had nothing to say and he wouldn't help her. She doubted that this attempt or any attempt would help either. In accordance with her words Sonya looked depressed, reluctant, and resigned. In contrast, she was stylishly dressed, had the gait of an athlete and a history of past and ongoing major scholastic and professional success. As manifestations of her depression she described crying herself to sleep every night and having to drag herself out of bed every morning, exhausted to face another day. She was refusing invitations from friends despite her loneliness.

Sonya regarded the years of her mother's treatment as having produced no apparent benefit. Her father thought psychiatry a pointless waste of money. The family difficulties centered on her disturbed brother, whose volcanic eruptions since infancy created the threat of constant havoc in the family. Both parents were overwhelmed by the disturbed child, the father avoidant, the mother hysterical. Sonya felt that she was both blamed for her brother's upsets and made responsible for calming either him or her mother or both. The older she became, the more her mother relied on her. She had had to give up her athletic pursuits in order to drive her brother to his psychiatrist to relieve her mother. This history emerged bit by bit over many months.

I was initially most impressed that this attractive and superbly educated young professional woman was profoundly depressed. I recommended psychotherapy twice a week and somewhat to my surprise, despite her pessimism, she accepted. I also suggested a consultation for antidepressant medication. This she resisted saying her mother had a bathroom full of drugs and they did no good. I acknowledged an understandable basis for her doubts. Nonetheless I insisted that she probably could be helped to suffer less while we worked to make sense of her experiences and their effect on her. She accepted the recommendation, began on a medication with moderate relief—what she called having a floor under her.

The therapy sessions quickly developed into a routine. Sonya would look at me with an expression of helpless despair and say nothing. I would ask, "How are you feeling?" She would answer, "Same." Remembering what she had said about her dreadful experience of silence in her previous treatment, I would ask about her sleep, her eating, her tiredness, what she was doing at work, how she had spent her weekend. She would respond with pertinent but terse answers. I believed, and thought she did as well, that the content here was less important than the effort we were both making to reduce the stress of a tense silent "empty" 45 minutes. My view was that I was tracking her responses as I would a traumatized infant with whom I was attempting to make and preserve contact despite the child's aversive withdrawal. I would observe her facial and postural cues and time my "interventions"—my questions and comments—to be within a range of her need to have an indication of my interested involvement. At the same time I tried hard to respect her aversion to intrusive demands for her to talk revealingly. She was attentive to my facial and postural expressions so that a great deal of nonverbal communication took place.

After a few weeks when it became clear she was "dutifully" coming regularly for sessions, I spontaneously began with "Same, same?" This small venture into variation was in keeping with patterns parents intuitively employ with infants to prevent their exchanges from becoming boringly repetitive. "Same, same?" was also my attempt to introduce a gentle touch of ironic humor and playfulness into the drab relentlessness of her depressive affect. She responded with the slightest indication of a twinkle, returned to her despondence, which I immediately acknowledged as the state of matters before us.

Several weeks later Sonya began to add a spontaneous comment to her lament about being exhausted and unable to bear it much longer. She might volunteer: "I won't be able to work this weekend." By following up on such remarks, she and I could learn about some activity that revealed her feelings, such as a wedding she hated going to because of the envy it aroused, or a visitor coming to stay with her and the cooking together she enjoyed.

After an hour in which we had a few moments of informative exchange, I would feel more hopeful until I discovered that often in the next hour she would take a full-blown plunge into depression and pessimism. I came to anticipate these sessions with dread. When in the session she would describe her despair, speaking in a tone as attuned to hers as I could, I would acknowledge her despair and pessimism. I would describe my understanding of the source of her despondency in her prior experiences, including the disappointing prior psychotherapy of her mother, brother, and herself. However, speaking from my own experience, I told her that I did not share her outlook that she was condemned to a lifelong depression. I stated that I was hopeful we could accomplish some alleviation of her suffering. I had to have a conviction of hopefulness, otherwise I would be uttering words of empty rhetoric. I felt that Sonya and I liked each other—that is, an intangible bond had been established, probably based largely on a reciprocal idealization. I admired the tenacity with which she used her abilities despite her problematic family life as well as the high professional standards she set for herself. I also believed she admired the tenacity of my professional stance with her and my skill in striking a balance between offering help and avoiding being intrusive.

My verbal communication with Sonya was constrained by her affect state, just as a mother's would be with a tantrum-prone child. But my communication with myself was open to verbal formulation of what I regarded as her message. I believed she was saying: "Will you take me at my word that I am dreadfully and miserably unhappy and allow *me*, not my mother and brother, to receive care, help, and concern rather than having to provide it to others?" I also believed she was saying, "No one helps me, everyone expects too much and no one wants to or can affect in the least the depressive gloom and doom I am resigned to." Further, I conjectured that the increasing frequency of her verbal communications and our easier dialogue indicated an increasing nonlinear attachment linkage.

Particularly at those moments I dreaded when Sonya's depression plunged into even greater despondency, I had to fall back on my inner monologue. I was confronted with the painful possibility that my faith that I ultimately could help her might be unsustainable. Her subtle hints at abandoning her treatment and less than subtle references to suicide added to my deeper perturbations. From my own early experiences, I had learned to sustain my equilibrium, even my sanity, while listening to the complaints of troubled people. I had inferred from many of these childhood experiences that I could have a positive effect on the troubled family member. This organizing principle played out successfully during the more stable depressed hours through my assumption that a positive nonverbal experience was being facilitated through my efforts—a "reward" of a sense of efficacy. Even during the "ordinary" depressed hours, small indications of a developing attachment plus an occasional exchange of ironic humor provided me with a sustaining mirroring vitalization.

But during the hours when Sonya's hopelessness seemed to be overwhelming her, my attunement could only lead me to a related feeling of helplessness. I sensed Sonya required me to appreciate fully her state of misery for her to be able to abandon her role reversal of caregiver to her family. I also sensed she distrusted thoroughly having me in the role of either benevolent caregiver or analytic explorer. Consequently, my empathic effort to be true to her affect state afforded *me* no sense of efficacy. My increasing feeling of being trapped and impotent led me to break from an empathic listening stance and fall back on a search within myself to reestablish my own perspective. I sought the basis for an expression of optimism about eventual help for her by reminding myself both of my successful experiences as psychiatrist-analyst and of this particular patient's many abilities and essential likeableness. To her I could say that I did not share her hopelessness without disconfirming the shared feeling of despair at the moment. From my knowledge of myself, I could recognize my own struggle against feeling helpless and unappreciated. My verbal statement of reassurance was probably as much a statement to myself as to Sonya.

When patients like Sonya offer little direct verbal communication, the most effective way to perceive and then elucidate verbally a perspective was through frequent moments of introspective awareness. My ability to perceive and describe the overt and unspoken process present in our exchange often offered Sonya the best opportunity to expand her awareness of her inner state. In addition, as the further exchanges illustrate, my intuitive loosely formulated introspection provided messages I delivered through comments, descriptions, and decisions that seemed simply to pop out of my mouth, what we have called "disciplined spontaneous engagements" (Lichtenberg, Lachmann, and Fosshage, 1996).

The loose coupling between verbal and nonverbal communication and linear and nonlinear cognition encourages an openness to spontaneity of feeling, word, and gesture. Humor, use of metaphor, model scene building, and some measured personal disclosures facilitate a vitalizing contrast to the dreary entrapment of an unrelenting aversive affective state. Special impact "relational moments" that result from spontaneity, surprise, and direct affective communication stand in sharp contrast to an impoverished pessimistic state of inner and outer communication. However, an analyst's less thought through spontaneity, that is, his flying by the seat of his pants, particularly with a traumatized patient, increases the risk of inadvertant retraumatization and increases the need for carefully tracking the sequences of associations and affective and gestural responses as they enter, become central, and then fade. Especially with a patient locked in an aversive pattern of negativism like Sonya, my only way to see myself through her eyes was to follow each subtle indicator based on largely nonverbal responses. Did the intervention lead to the tiniest flicker of interest and vitality or was it followed by eye aversion and silent withdrawal? Did my interventions, when tracked over an hour, a week, a month or more, appear to mount in effectiveness by eliciting an increasingly collaborative response?

During one hour Sonya stated that this was a bad time for her. I wondered if she was using a euphemism for a menstrual period and decided to venture a direct question. She blushed, gave a slight indication of a giggle, and answered that she did not have periods. It was a bad time since the weather prevented her from taking her daily early morning run. She added the new information that with her running and her very controlled vegetarian diet, she had learned to prevent periods. Her way of providing this information implied that further questions would be unwelcome. The underlying principle of our "communication" was that we could provide openings to each other for sharing revelations as long as my interventions did not place me in an argumentative opposition to her commitment to pessimism.

In another session, Sonya noted she had not had time to buy any new clothes for some time. Since I found her clothing exceptionally attractive and varied, I told her I was surprised because she dressed so well. She snapped back, "My father would only say I spend too much." She shut off further inquiry at this time, but I concluded she was comparing me with her father—probably outside of awareness. At a later time, when she was talking about an expenditure, I asked about her father's tightness. No, she said he wasn't tight, he had paid for her whole education. He did what he promised unlike her mother who had never come to visit her. Mother excused herself saying her psychiatrist had told her she had interfered too much in her daughter's life, and she now wanted to give her more independence. Father was coming to visit, but Sonya wasn't looking forward to it since father's wife would be coming, and she would have to be nice to her despite her dislike. Along with her mother, she blamed her father's wife for the disruption of the family, and for her never being able to be alone with father. This information was provided in one or two sentences volunteered during moments of sharing.

A few months later, Sonya had cancelled the prior session to take her professional boards. She entered casually dressed, perfunctorily asked how I was, and looked away depressed and exhausted. I noted her tired, sad appearance. She said the boards were awful, she didn't know how she did, and she didn't care. After a silence, I asked if going back to work was troubling her. She answered she had decided to take the day off. She couldn't face work. I told her I was glad to see she was trying to look after herself. I recalled that last week she had taken over for others requiring her to work late into the night. As she often did when I was on the wrong track, Sonya corrected me. She said, "It's not work, it's the boards. My work can give me a feeling of accomplishment; taking the boards gives me none." Following her lead, I asked what the experience of taking the boards had been like? In a more open manner, she went on to describe the two six-hour days, the nature of the questions, and her struggles with them. In a rare reference to me as a person, she ended by saying: "It was as if you had to learn the names of all the state capitols in alphabetical order to pass your medical boards."

A: Oh.

P: It was stupid!

A: A frustrating, unnecessary exercise.

P: I called several friends and they were empathetic, but it was my own fault—not taking the waiver when I could and transferring the boards I had taken [previously] and passed. I feel like I was hit by a stick. It's all so stupid. Being asked a lot of stuff you don't need to know. Being kept in a room for two days.

A: It sounds like torture.

P: Umhum [looking away silently].

A: Only you said "hit by a stick"—did you mean punished?

P: [With a burst of anger] What else would it mean?

A: It could mean abuse.

P: Oh. Well it was both—abuse and punishment.—What are you smiling about? [I had smiled involuntarily and she asked in a way that seemed genuinely curious as well as provocative.]

A: I like it when you flare up. You come alive, you become animated, and for a moment you are out of your despair.

P: Well, maybe I should be a smartass more.

A: I know you can be lively with your friends.

P: I try.

A: Do you have to try or sometimes does your liveliness just flow.

P: Sometimes it flows but mostly I try.
[A silence followed in which I felt that we had exhausted that topic and she could take over initiating.]

P: I had a good experience with my mother. A surprise. She sent me flowers before the boards and called to wish me luck. She never calls. It was nice of her.

A: You were surprised and pleased.

P: I didn't expect to hear from anyone. Of course I didn't tell my father.

A: What went into your decision not to tell him.

P: I knew he'd say, "How many times did I tell you to apply for the waiver." I didn't want to hear it.

A: You had been hitting yourself with the stick enough—Your mother was thinking of your feelings, your father of his advice.

P: (Defensively) He doesn't know me. I was only a little kid [when he left]. He'll ask me about it after a while.

In this hour I could recognize a pattern emerging. I would mention to Sonya a negative reference to her father's "tightness" in order to invite her further thoughts and feelings. She would counter it with a positive statement. The same existed for her mother. I formed the hypothesis that she was responding in a fashion common to children of divorced parents. The child harbors grievances toward each parent but feels she must defend each parent against the vehement blaming of the other. By defending either parent against the other parent's criticisms, the child prevents herself from being pulled into an alliance that will cost her her attachment to either father or mother. In fact I later learned that Sonya carefully doled out phone calls and visits to mother and father, regardless of the inconvenience to herself. Forming this hypothesis led me to another question—whether or not to bring it up in the hour. I chose not to do so. I based my decision on my conclusion that, while I was interested in exploring patterns and their meanings, Sonya was as yet neither interested in, nor open to wondering about, the whats and whys of her actions. I was beginning to feel confident she was getting there but also believed premature efforts would be more hindrance than help.

As fall began, Sonya began to be more depressed. She associated this with seasonal changes. She knew about the therapeutic use of "lights" but reiterated her pessimism that nothing would help. One hour when she was particularly depressed, I asked her about her medication. She answered that she was taking it but it was not helping. I suggested she call the neuropharmacologist and reevaluate the choice of medication. She objected and we sat in a stalemated silence. As I looked over to her, our eyes met and I reacted facially to her painful expression. She asked me "What?" referring to my look. I answered sympathetically, "You look like a sad little kitten." This was a metaphor I had never used before. A few moments later she answered:

P: I'll go but I don't want to.
A: I know you feel pessimistic with your mother having a medicine chest full of drugs and no benefit and your connecting taking medicine with being sick and hating to think of yourself as sick. Is there something else?
P: I don't like Dr. N. I don't want to go back to him.
A: You don't have to go back to him. I can refer you to someone else.
P: O.K.
A: Dr. H (Her number is . . .)

Sonya went to Dr. H and was put on another antidepressant. Within two weeks she experienced a major mood shift.

P: Your won't believe it but I have a big crush.
A: Oh (pleased to see her looking happy and exuberant).
P: On Patrick Rafter (an Australian tennis player who had just unexpectedly won the U.S. Open). Ann called and said, 'The minute I saw him I knew he'd be a guy you'd go for. And I've arranged with our client to meet him."

Sonya was introduced to him and went to a party with the tennis players. She also moved into an apartment and furnished it with carefully selected items. Several hours later she announced that she had another surprise for me. She had gotten a kitten. To satisfy my curiosity I asked her if she remembered my describing her as looking like a sad little kitten and she answered no. I was surprised and puzzled by my choice of metaphor and remained so until a long time later when I described the experience to a colleague. She insisted I had unconsciously recognized that Sonya and I were engaged in something akin to play with a kitten. I didn't resonate with this suggestion, thinking I had always had dogs and knew little about kittens. The next day I was shocked to remember that at a time when one of my daughters was going through a troubled time she had insisted on having a kitten of her own. We had gotten her an adorable little marmalade kitten that in the midst of a house move had gotten out and been killed— a very troubling memory filled with guilt, remorse, and sadness. My reference to a kitten I believe was a condensation of my daughter's unhappy face and the run-over kitten, a communication of caring and deep concern.

Over the next weeks she described the kitten awakening her at 4 A.M. wanting to play and scratching playfully at her eye lashes. She also gave a vivid depiction of the kitten shivering in terror on being taken to the vets for a third sulfur bath for ringworm.

She began to appear mildly depressed. I asked if she had been in touch with Dr. H about her medication. She had not since Dr. H had asked her to get blood tests and she was extremely reluctant to go for the procedure. I was reminded of her depiction of the shivering kitten and asked her about her feeling.

P: I went to an orthodontist from the time I was 9 until I was 13. It was horrible! I hated him. I told my mother I didn't want to go to him but she wouldn't listen. She wouldn't send me to someone else. I really hated him.

A: Was it the pain of the procedures or something you sensed about him?

P: I don't remember what it was like. . . . He went to jail.

A: For what?

P: For molesting little girls.

A: Do you . . .

P: (Interrupting) I don't know. I don't remember. The newspaper said about 15 girls came forward.

The next hour I asked if we could return to what she had mentioned. She reiterated that she didn't remember anything but hating him. All she knew was that her mother had told her. Her mother had said that when she and Sonya discovered the news-paper account, Sonya had told her that he didn't put the instruments on the table but on her chest. I asked what that might have felt like when he would touch her changing body. She answered she didn't remember telling her mother that either. At this point I decided a facet of the general aversiveness to open communication that had been present from the beginning of her treatment probably involved her being dissociated and detached during stressful situations. In response to my inquiry, Sonya revealed she did not remember events at all. She only remembered broad generalizations. She did not think in event scenes or images. She could not imagine herself into what she might have felt as a pre-teen with the orthodontist. I conjectured to myself that her revelation about the orthodontist pointed to an enacted exchange with me when, unlike her mother, I accepted her decision to shift from the male neuropharmacologist she expressed dislike for to a female she felt safer with. I further believed that her gaps in memory would make an interpretation of this connection meaningless to her.

To this point in our exchanges, she had evidenced no spontaneous curiosity, no reflecting back on any experience to wonder about it. I had carried the full weight of evoking interest in whatever aspect of her life she was willing to tell me about. The progress was mainly in her increasing openness to reveal aspects of her current life and to drop in references to the past.

Gradually Sonya's general outlook had become more positive despite overwork and fatigue. In the hour that follows she appeared more glum and uncommunicative than she had been for some time. I reviewed my memory of the previous hours and finding no trigger I recognized, I returned to asking Sonya questions to elicit a hint of the source for the disruption. Her monosyllabic answers brought us to a silence, and I made no further attempt to elicit response. After a considerable pause, as often happened, Sonya, responding less to my ineffectualness than to my prior concerned effort, volunteered that it was her birthday. To my look of surprise she said "What"? I answered "Oh you look so glum and birthdays are usually a time of celebration."

P: You wouldn't think so if your brother ruined every birthday you had.

A: I guess I wouldn't.

P: He'd throw a tantrum. He couldn't stand to have the focus be on me.

A: He'd come to your party?

P: Of course. You look skeptical. Maybe you would have thought of something to do with him but my mother never did. She was too afraid of him to tell him not to come or to behave.

A: And your father?

P: He was too busy.

A: [After a pause] And today, what will you do?

P: Nothing. I don't want anyone to know.

A: Me?

P: You—anybody. What's the use? [Long pause with head down that ended by her looking up.]

A: Where did you go?

P: My mother called to wish me a happy birthday. I told her there was nothing happy about it. She said [using a haughty chilling theatrical voice] "Well, it was the happiest day of my life." I told her that's fine for her but it doesn't affect me. "Don't blame me if you are unhappy." [In a supercilious tone] "I've learned, you have to be responsible for your own happiness."

A: Nothing inviting or mutual, only a continuation of the contention.

P: My father will send a card with a check.

A: Again nothing that feels like a personal connection.

P: He can't be bothered to buy something for me and wouldn't know what to get me if he did. He insists on celebrating my birthday with his wife's and I won't go home for that.

A: Their sensitivity to your desire for a celebration of your "day," shared with your family, feels sadly missing.

P: What sensitivity? My mother thinks only of herself and my father doesn't think at all. He only follows his routine.

A: And me?

P: There's nothing you can do. You're not my parents.

A: I can at least try to be sensitive to your feelings, the way you are to the people at work who ask you to help, and with your friends.

P: [After a long pause] How come if they are so insensitive, I'm so sensitive?

A: [After a short pause] I've wondered that too. We really don't know. Your memories are so protectively limited. For example, we don't know about other people who may have been there for you.

P: Other people? There was no one.

A: No one in your house?

P: Other than Janet.

A: Janet?

P: She was the housekeeper so mother could work. She was there all the time as far back as I know until I was a teenager. Do you think Janet could have been important? [Pause]

A: Yes. It's possible.

P: [Then with a shift in affect state] Oh, I didn't tell you, my old roommate called and insisted that she and her husband would take me out for dinner for my birthday. We made a pact that we would hate birthdays together.

[At the door I asked Sonya if it was OK for me to wish her a happy birthday, to which she responded with a nod and a self-conscious smile.]

An analysis of the subtle shifts in communication during this hour illustrates verbal and nonverbal cues that tilt the dialogue in the direction of attachment building, enactment, or exploration. Recognizing her altered mood and uncommunicativeness, I first attempted to discover the source of her disrupted state. When my effort failed, I was faced with a choice both conceptual and practical. On an action level, I could attempt to placate, soothe, encourage, or prod Sonya, none of which I felt would be effective. Conceptually, I could regard the stalemated pause we had created as a failure of my empathy or her cooperativeness. Or I could regard the pause and the tension we both felt as a welcome opportunity for a spontaneous communication to arise. My tilt toward a positive expectation was supported by the current solidity of our relations which contrasted greatly with the fragile bond of our early sessions.

Sonya broke the silence with her startling announcement of her birthday and inquired about my facial expression. A quick spontaneous back-and-forth dialogue followed. I began by answering her question about the thought behind my facial expression. She then made a rare connection between the past—her brother's disruptiveness—and the present—her sour feeling about birthdays. This exchange which began as an enactment then opened into an inquiry about her parents' failures with her brother. I then attempted to move the inquiry to include her view of me. Was I being experienced as a repetition of past negative expectations and, if so, was I similar to mother or father? Was I being viewed in a more positive light and, if so, analogous to whom? Sonya's answer—you—anybody—what's the use—brought us to another impasse. I regarded her looking up after a long silence as a cue to reconnect and asked "where did you go?" as an open-ended inquiry. She resumed expressing her feelings about her parents and accepted my comments on her disappointment. Again my inquiry about her placement of me in association to the parental dissapointments brought us to her enigmatic statement, "You're not my parents." I was unsure of exactly what she meant. My guess was she was saying "You and I have no biological-familial connection. If I were to acknowledge my positive feelings for you, I would have to experience desires that I don't want to have stirred." I positioned myself as I saw myself with her in the here and now, believing her cues were telling me further inquiry would be fruitless. Then Sonya broke this mini-impasse with an unusual (for her) shift into an exploratory motivation indicated by her "How come?"

I offered a spontaneous intuitive inquiry/suggestion about "other people." At the time I could not have documented the source of my particular wondering. On reflection after the hour I recognized a parallel in my own life of the positive source of sensitivity servants and nonfamily members had provided. At the time neither Sonya nor I could know whether Janet has been a source of secure attachment based on mutual empathic sensitivity. A possible confirmation could be derived from the positive affective shift Sonya experienced as the hour was coming to an end. She suddenly remembered, "Oh, I didn't tell you" of the anticipated dinner. With the recall of her positive expectation based on her twinship sharing with her friend who had pledged to hate birthdays with her, the repeated negative "anyone" or "anybody" was replaced for that moment. Her emotional shift permitted the enactment about my place in the hierarchy of parent-friend-anybody incorporated in the final, playful, ironic exchange: "Is it OK if I wish you a happy birthday?"

Metaphors and Model Scenes

Communication combines relating and exploring. When we communicate with others and with ourselves we make connections—conscious and out of awareness, linear and nonlinear, implicit and explicit. We cannot learn to relate effectively with others or ourselves without affective communication. In this chapter we are taking up an aspect of the question "Why talk?" We first demonstrated the power of words as designators that help mother and baby, analyst and analysand to focus attention on the essential feature of an intention, a motive. We next considered how word, gesture, and metaphor flow back and forth in a clinical exchange with one or the other assuming a leading role at any given moment. In this flow analyst and analysand build a relationship, learn intuitively how to connect affectively, how to move from verbal and gestural empathic perspective to enactment and back to empathy. In all our examples we emphasize both an attachment motive and an exploratory motive. The relationship makes possible a sense of safety that makes possible an exploration as well as providing the principal datum of the inquiry. In turn the exploration contributes to the openness and flexibility of attachments. Metaphor and model scenes provide particular communicative tools for integrating relational connecting and exploratory connecting.

In *Mapping the Mind*, Levin notes that metaphors "surprise the listener in part because of their novelty. The improbable and therefore unexpected combination of ideas, sensory modalities, meanings and so forth arouses the patients's interest, without it I do not believe synthetic activity can occur" (1991, p. 6). Levin notes that when metaphors are offered naturally without artifice they treat with respect the patient's intelligence and maximize the informational value of the message. Their ambiguity allows "for simultaneous relevance at multiple levels of experience and meaning" (p. 8). Metaphors arouse activity in the left hemisphere linguistically and the right hemisphere nonlinguistically, and "thus come close to being simultaneous translations of themselves" (p. 29).

Metaphors thus fit perfectly into conversational exchanges that are being conducted in a spirit of inquiry. We can illustrate the application of metaphor in the clinical examples used in this chapter of "dodging" and "sad little kitten."

"Dodging": Supervisor and analytic trainee were exploring together the successes of the supervisee's empathic perceptions while having in the back of their minds an openness to recognize and construct other possible meanings. The supervisor's recognition of the trainee's having drifted unaware into the patient's pattern of avoidance could have been described more prosaicly. Via the metaphor of "dodging," however, an unexpected novelty was introduced that conveyed maximal information. The ambiguity of the metaphor in turn permitted the analytic trainee to recognize the fit both to himself in that he was "dodging" what his patient was doing, and to his patient in the latter's avoidance of facing up to the implications of events she was relating. The patient then demonstrated her highly skilled capacity to both absorb information that would reveal herself to herself and employ her own metaphors to expand their shared understanding. Her acknowledgment of the experiential accuracy of "dodging" took the form of two metaphors of her own "skirting around the edges" and "dance around." Interspersed between these two metaphors the patient told about her father and her neighbor Jane during which time she and the analyst brought to light a prime example of what she dodged—her need to be a caregiver and comforter.

In her spontaneous choice of her own metaphors, the patient may have presented herself and her analyst with word pictures that had more impact than the one chosen by the supervisor. Possibly skirting and dancing were more personal, even feminine, to her than the male supervisor's choice.

The hour contains yet another thread. While patient and analyst were ardently carrying forward an exploration, the subject had subtly shifted from avoidance to her need to be a caregiver, thereby providing another potential enactment of dodging. After a pregnant pause the analyst brought the two of them back to the primary focus by utilizing a model scene that suddenly came to the analyst's mind. With the open space to creativity, the pause, and her association to the dodged, skirted, and danced around cigarette and drug usage provided, she entered the scene directly: "Clarisse, have you been smoking? What is going on that you are so upset?" Here we have startle and confrontation, an immediacy of communicative thrust. The unforeseeable result could have been a spark of immediate affective resonance or a disruption and provocation. Happily it was the former as the patient welled up with the activated memory of how painful her parents' not asking had been.

Model scenes, we suggest, are extended metaphors with great power to arouse affective recognition in ways that move the analytic inquiry forward. Just as metaphors appeal to the portions of the brain that process multiple modalities verbally and imagistically, a model scene invites reentrant signaling from multiple sources. The model scene of the patient smoking and experimenting with drugs, ashamed and terrified to tell her parents, but deeply desirous of their interest and help, leaving a trail of smoke odors and painfully hurt that she wasn't asked, touches on images, verbal communications, and deeply felt affects. So how does it work to bring about positive change? Each lived experience of significance leads children or adults to make inferences about themselves and others. For Clarisse we can assume one inference she drew was: "I don't have to face problems of my own that arouse shame or fear, and no one will recognize the problems I avoid and help me to deal with them. Also, I am not to make others face problems but to be a caregiver to them." This schema or map acts as a category of experience, so that close repetitions add consistency to the expectation that avoidance is a relatively fixed organized and organizing pattern. Divergences such as the analyst's interpretation of dodging are appraised by the brain as violations of the category leading to recategorization. Recategorization is apt to involve some alteration in the relatively fixed map and additionally to reentrant signaling, forging links to maps of other experiences during which avoidances were faced or help in confronting and solving problems was forthcoming. The cognitive attentional focus that resulted from "dodging" exposed the discrepancy between what Clarisse and the analyst each thought she and he were doing and what they came to recognize they were doing. This recognition and further associations to the metaphor provided the stimulus for two new scenes—one with Clarisse's father and one with her neighbor Jane. Each were affective scenes that would be played out as skirting and dancing around or being direct and confrontative.

In addition, another scene of even greater immediacy arose from the experience itself of the enactment of the analyst directly helping the patient to confront the avoided. What did the model scene add to this effect? First, the analyst's reference to the smoking odor bridged the present, with its more tempered emotion of shame, and the past with its more emotionally intense mixture of shame, tears, and pain. Bringing the old map with its inferences and expectations into the immediacy of the present offers the patient an excellent opportunity for recategorization. Second, the analyst's confrontive enactment "Clarisse, have you been smoking? What is going on?" elicited an immediate affective experience—a powerful new map to appraise against the old. Third, the process involved in analyst and analysand together working with the model scene creates a map of an empathically organized attachment experience to appraise against the essentially negative expectations of past empathic failures. Model scenes work not only because they tap in on past significant events but because they are taken up by analysand and analyst as joint properties or shared stories to be amended, added to, and reflected on. The manner in which analyst and analysand employ model scenes as valued tools in pursuit of the exploration of the meaning of past and current lived experiences feeds into the sense of uniqueness of the analytic relationship. The model scene and its radiating stories are comparable to aspects of family myths such as when we met, or the time we were stranded during the hurricane. The possessors of the myth draw together as they share and amend the story line and apply it to their present.

In the example of Sonya, the analyst's metaphoric expression "sad little kitten" became elaborated through an image implicitly equating Sonya's sadness and helplessness with a kitten needing rescue and mothering. Unlike model scenes that are developed by analyst and patient through verbal exchanges, this model scene was developed partly by accessing experiences from the analyst's and Sonya's past. Then, further elaboration evolved from a series of enactments. The analyst's descriptive labelling of his response to Sonya's depressive state seemed to him to come from nowhere but he later recognized that it derived from a traumatic memory involving his daughter's kitten's death. The unpredictable effect was that the descriptor touched so many scenes in Sonya's present, past, and future life. The present effect was for Sonya to feel empathically touched, thereby countering her pessimistic expectation that her needs would never be attended to. The immediate recategorization led to her acceptance of the recommendation of medication. The next surprise was Sonya's buying a kitten, and with that act a series of elaborations on the model scene began. In a treatment so sparing in communication, the ensuing dialogue focused on the kitten became crucial. From the past, we drew understanding from her memory of her brother's abuse of the family cat and his intense dependence on the pet, which mirrored his abuse of her and his past and continuing dependence on her. In both instances, the identification of Sonya with the family cat opened a channel exposing her troubled feelings. In contrast, Sonya now formed new maps in her relationship with her new kitten, whose attachment to her provided a much needed source of joy. Her sharing of her experiences with the kitten shivering with fear, eagerly greeting her each night when she came home, snuggling against her, and awakening her playfully facilitated an implicit nonverbalized linkage of these affectionate vitalizing experiences with the analyst as intimately connected. In this atypical analysis, an atypical model scene offered reappraisal, recategorization, and reentrant possibilities similar to the more directly cocreated model scene applications we have discussed in previous publications (Lichtenberg, 1989; Lachmann and Lichtenberg, 1992).

CHAPTER SEVEN

VERBAL AND NONVERBAL
COMMUNICATION DURING ANALYSIS

"The message contains the message" (Lichtenberg, Lachmann, and Fosshage, 1996, pp. 94–95). This principle of technique places communication in the center of our approach to psychoanalytic therapy. What the message consists of has been the subject of each of our clinical chapters. We have considered spontaneity and flexibility in moment-to-moment exchanges in chapter 3. The dynamism of words, feelings, and enacted interplay that moves implicit and explicit memory and relatively rigid relational schemas toward positive change was discussed in chapter 4. In chapter 5, we addressed the silent but powerful influence of past relational configurations. We described the body as both a direct voice and a proxy voice for more emotional expressiveness. We focused in chapter 6 on the careful reading of gesture required when verbal communication is blotted out by an overwhelming affect state.

In this chapter we will follow patient and analyst through different stages of a complete analysis. We will illustrate the changing emphasis on the message conveyed by verbal and nonverbal communications. With Mrs. S, the patient whose successful analysis we describe, words both conveyed and disrupted meaningful communication. At times the major message was discerned through patient-analyst enactments and role responses on the part of the analyst. At other times the key to an exploration of the message arose from the patient's affect state or from metaphors in dreams and associations or from vocal tone—the "music" more than the "lyrics."

These statements imply that the flow of a message is like a linear passage from patient to analyst or analyst to patient. Even though it is often difficult to illustrate in the course of an analysis, analyst and patient are continuously influencing what is being said implicitly and explicitly. Each partner organizes outer speech with the other in mind and whatever revenants from the past he or she may be addressing unconsciously. Even more important, each partner carries forward a continuous inner monologue-dialogue. Depending on whether the other is sensed as empathically response or critical and unsafe, the content of inner speech will be spoken aloud with more or less censoring. Ultimately, the forward movement of the analysis depends on the persistent maintenance of a spirit of inquiry despite obfuscations in the verbal and nonverbal communications we illustrate in the analysis of Mrs. S.

The First Week of Mrs S's Analysis

Mrs. S began her analysis as if she were a runaway train. Through rapid, pressured speech she gave a convincing account of her childhood and adolescent attachment to her father. Through the first three hours of this barrage of speech and information, I felt shut out by the absence of conversational pauses and puzzled by the meaning of the vocal pattern. I assumed that the relevance of the information meant that she was intact cognitively and that during her interrupted prior analysis, she had acquired considerable knowledge of the impact of her relationship to her father and his tragic death.

In the last hour of the first week, she described feeling as if she were jumping into a well. Responding to the tension I sensed from her pressured speech plus the disturbing nature of the content she was relating, I suggested she might be trying to jump into a well of deep problems at a time when I could be of only limited help. She said that made sense—it would be as if she were continuing with her previous analyst, and the five-year interruption had not occurred. She then said that I should be grateful for her deep stuff. She felt angry and like clamming up. I asked her to tell me more about the source of her feeling, and she responded that she felt rejected. Then, in an unpressured way, she filled in important details of her history.

Combined with what she had told me in the consultative hours, I now knew that a period of anxiety, dread, and depression had led to her initially entering treatment. Her mind had raced out of control, and she had the illusion of seeing dead bodies. This partial decompensation had followed a sequence of traumatic events. Her father had died in an automobile crash. Circumstances were highly suggestive that he had suicidal intent. While still reeling from her father's death, she discovered that the man with whom she had been living since her college days was having an affair with another woman. Her mother, to whom she turned at this time, provided little help, and Mrs. S drifted into a brief chaotic romance with a man her father's age. Subsequently she began psychotherapy with an analyst with whom she formed an immediate sustaining relationship. While in treatment, she met and married an affectionate, capable man who was successful in a business similar to her father's. After three years of psychotherapy, she began a year of analysis, which was interrupted when her husband's work required him to go overseas for two years. She managed the separation from the analyst, the birth of a daughter, and the time away without undue functional regression or disturbance in her sense of self. A few minutes before the end of the hour she said she felt her tone was off key. She wanted me to accept her dipping into her well of sorrow. She felt she had always had to show her father only her happy face. I suggested that she wanted to feel free to show me all her feelings, and she agreed.

Discussion 1

What did Mrs. S's message contain about the strategy she established to preserve her attachment to a significant caregiver? Borrowing from linguistic patterns found in the Adult Attachment

Interview, we believe that her involement with the losses of her father and prior analyst interferred with her monitoring her discourse for its accessibility as a communication (Hesse and Main, 2000). This places her squarely in the group of preoccupied speakers and suggests a behavioral origin as a child who both anxiously approached and then pushed away her caregiver. Mrs. S followed a comparable pattern in her anxious desire to remain in and reestablish her analysis while postponing beginning with me for a year after having made an initial contact.

Mrs. S's message presented a paradox as a communication to an analyst. She collaborated in the task of expressing freely a seemingly close approximation of her inner state, that is, following the "rule" of free association. However, she was not collaborative in the ordinary sense of offering an intelligible participant communication with a listener-responder. Exchanges between dyadic partners are collaborative when symbolic elaborations in words are slow and sequential, containing pauses that permit the reply of the other. They follow the pattern of I speak to you, then you respond, and in turn I respond to your response. In contrast, Mrs. S's volume, tone, rhythm, and tempo worked both to preclude a dyadic sharing and to eliminate awareness of my "absence." In the absence of turn taking, even the connection through "ums" and "I sees," I could not track the nature of any beginning coconstruction until my direct intervention in the fourth hour.

The major impact of her message conveyed the dominance of the aversive motivational system. The intensity of her anxious pressured affect made me question whether she was in or near a panic state in which cognitive coherence would become totally lost. I sensed a need to establish my presence, whether in the sense of providing containment for her distress or regulation for her communicative style.

Information is communicated through parallel systems of explicit verbal explications of current and past experience and implicit enactive renderings (Lyons-Ruth, 1999). The message at the explicit verbal level of Mrs. S's overstimulating mode of interactional relationship with her father was conveyed strongly in its enactive form of excitement, confusion, and loss. When the explicit verbal dimension of a patient's communication predominates, the analyst is more likely to process in inner speech conceptual understanding and then verbalize a selected offering of his assumptions about the patient's state of mind and its meaning. However, when, as with Mrs. S, the implicit enactive mode of relating predominates, the analyst is more likely to be puzzled about what is taking place between them and to be pulled inexorably into an interactional form of role response.

In the fourth hour the nature of the verbal exchanges helped delineate the enactive roles. "Jumping into a well of sorrow" defined her as an abandoned lover in need of rescue. The explicit clarity of this message opened for me an opportunity to convey my understanding of our relative positions. I suggested that my reading of her state of mind was of wanting to plunge (recklessly?) into problems and my response to be one of wanting to advise caution lest I, in my puzzled state, prove to be an ineffective rescuer. She responded by calming and identifying the real object of her discourse—her previous analyst. Mrs. S remembered him as open to her distress in all its intensity, whereas, I, seeing my role as "calmer," became her father demanding her happy face. In the rapid pace of these exchanges, important background information was conveyed verbally, but more salient was what we conveyed through transactions about who we were to each other in the dynamic here and now. Thus began a process of her learning explicitly what she needed to tell me about who she was to herself and who I was to her, and her learning how to relate to me to get what she needed from me. And thus began also a process of my learning explicitly what she needed to hear from and about me and my learning implicitly how to relate to her to be able to do what I needed to do to maintain the duality of relating and exploring. Our implicit and explicit learning processes might converge as they did in the fourth hour and diverge as they did repeatedly throughout the analysis.

A significant message was contained in Mrs. S's acknowledgment that she felt her moments of unpressured informative speech to be off key. This remark conveyed a reflective ability to monitor her emotion (her calmed state), to evaluate its impact on her (an accommodative false self), and to convey her aversion with a welcome directness. That she could be reflectively aware of her change in tone and its dystonic feel to her meant that she could both acknowledge and verbalize her inner state. This demonstration of reflective capacity indicated that she could function at a higher level of consciousness when an empathically based "holding environment" had been established, and thus provided encouragement to our beginning work.

The First Year

During the first 10 months of her analysis, she returned regularly to past traumatic events. She felt that throughout her childhood and adolescence she and her father had established a contract to be and remain special to each other. In choosing to live with another man, she believed she and her father felt she had been unfaithful to him, and she blamed herself for his death. After his death, she wanted to replace him first with the older man and then with her first analyst. Following the interruption of the analysis, she had symbolically kept in touch with the analyst by continuing her analysis in her mind.

Toward me, she felt competitive. She wanted to show off and constantly gain my approval. She stated that she was performing as Scheherazade, filling me with 1,001 tales so that I would not be bored and replace her with a more interesting patient. If I spoke to any of her frequent, insightful reflections, she would agree with my comment, offer further confirmation, and begin the familiar process of verbal barrage. Comments about her excitable reaction led only to hurt feelings of being unappreciated but brought no change in the pattern.

I was concerned that my interventions were contributing to her overexcited states, but I knew that not addressing her material would not be helpful. I was convinced, as was she, that we had come to understand many sources for her having become overstimulated as a child. The household revolved around the tension between her parents. Her father, an ambitious executive, wanted his wife to entertain in order to further his career. She refused, ridiculed his pretentions, and frequently humiliated him by getting drunk at parties.

As a little girl Mrs. S had moved into the breach between her parents. She had memories of her father lying around nude. He would neck with her and joke that he owned her marriage contract. When her father was away for extended periods, she became mother's companion, sat with her as she bathed, and climbed into bed with her.

Mrs. S's memory of her work with her first analyst was that he had frequently asked for details about her sexual problems in order to help her overcome her almost total frigidity. Whenever he questioned her, she felt him to be like a powerful penetrator— as forceful and marvelous a man as her father. She was pleased if I appeared to act in this manner with her, but would then react with overexcitement.

Alternatively, if I seemed to be unresponsive, her rate of speech would slow down. She complained of being unable to think. She felt tired, fogged out, without vitality. She became drowsy and occasionally fell asleep briefly. When I tried to help her see the connections I believed existed between my diminished activity and her clamming up, she might agree in a listless way or ignore me. In any case, my interventions had no noticeable effect.

In the tenth month, she began an hour by telling me about a dream she had in which she decided to use her basement for a child's playroom. Her associations led me to ask if the dream might refer to thoughts of touching or playing around her "basement" or bottom. She recalled (material she had previously related) that in college her principal means of stimulating herself had been by wiping around her anus. She had developed a perianal itch and had scratched herself until she bled. She added, in passing, that her mother had frequently given her enemas. She then reverted to the familiar pattern of talking rapidly and excitedly. Her thoughts became more loosely connected—images of people merged indistinctly, and the thread of what she said became difficult or impossible to follow. I found myself experiencing a familiar feeling of confusion and frustration.

I reflexively said to myself, 'Oh, shit!' Then I heard what I had said to myself and in a rapid-fire way associated: shit—enemas

—barrage of words—looser and looser content. With these associations as a springboard, I postulated that she was trying to express to me that the enemas and the attendant interaction with her mother had played a significant organizing influence in her childhood. I hoped that insight into her enema experience would provide a key to understanding an unrecognized motivation in her transference to me.

I suggested to her that in some way she might be reexperiencing through her excited barrage of words something akin to the buildup and explosion of tension and contents during an enema. She responded seriously to this suggestion and without additional excitement. She described how her mother asked her daily if she had a bowel movement. If she said yes, nothing would happen. But if she said no or hesitated, she would be given an enema. Mother gave herself an enema daily. The hour ended with the sharing of this information.

With the patient's initiative and cooperation the theme of the enema experiences occupied the center of the analysis for the next 10 weeks. Based on her current reactions, I described what I imagined the enema experience had been like. She described memories of trying to hold back the contents of the enema and finally exploding forth. She was afraid to displease her mother but would become very excited. She would lie to her mother about having a BM to avoid an enema. From this description of the struggle in the bathroom I inferred that she had felt anger toward her mother for giving her the enemas, and that a similar feeling of anger had exploded forth toward me through her barrage of words. For the first time since my initial interpretation of the significance of her enema experience, she interrupted our joint effort to reconstruct their memory and meaning. She took up the idea of anger and again became overexcited, giving out with a rush of increasingly disconnected associations about being angry.

I again felt bewildered and my attention momentarily turned inward. I recognized that I felt a mild sense of irritation, and I conjectured that I had interpreted her experience not primarily from within her state of mind but from my own. I postulated that I had based my assessment of the importance for her of anger in her experiences with the enemas on the irritation I had felt as the target of her verbal overload. I had rationalized this inaccurate construction by assuming her reaction to be the angry struggle children commonly experience over having their bodies intruded upon (an issue that was to come up later). I recalled that she had told me she was asked about her BMs each day and concluded that obviously it was she who controlled the frequency of the enemas. I then conjectured that her reactivated resistance might be a response to my failure to continue to understand her inner feelings and thoughts after so promising a beginning.

I asked Mrs. S if her excited talking might have been stimulated by her feeling that I had failed to understand her true feelings about the enemas when I had emphasized her anger. She did not respond directly, but in a calmer fashion acknowledged that she remembered having welcomed the enemas. She had regarded them as indicating that her mother cared about her enough to do something active. I was now able to help her reconstruct a view of her family life considerably different from the one she had previously presented. Before, she had portrayed her father as her lover who courted her with such gallantries as "You name it, honey, and I'll get if for you. Anything, anything at all." Now she said that these promises were generally hollow, like some of her insights and "agreements" with my suggestions. As she did with me, her father would get instantly excited about any suggestion she would make, but he did not follow through in a practical way. Most important, he failed to help her curb outbursts of outrageous behavior with effective discipline. I interpreted that the significance of the enemas was that their administration meant to her that, contrary to her father, her mother had tried to impose order. Mother's method—the enemas—was indeed faulty, but it was "real" in comparison. Bit by bit, we reconstructed one set of feelings the enemas gave her. They made her feel all cleaned out, her anger washed away, her wildness dampened down, and her guilt reduced with the fantasy she was being punished for her misdeeds. But most of all, the fact of mother's giving them to her imparted a feeling of importance—of really mattering to someone.

The effect of this analytic work was measurably to increase our sense of effectively working together. It facilitated the transition from a difficult opening phase to a productive, middle phase of treatment.

Discussion 2

How do we discern initial indicators of change in a message that has become established, repetitive, and seemingly inflexible? When the message contains a highly organized strategy for preserving an attachment how can we recognize a shift from one strategy or attachment person to another? Attachment research finds that infants can employ different patterns of attachment to different caregivers, for example, an avoidant attachment to an unresponsive mother and a secure attachment to a father sensitive to the child's needs. However, as reflected by the AAI, adults will reveal one dominant state of mind with respect to attachment rather than well defined multiplicity. This coincides with the common finding during analysis of a dominant transference, say to the mother, a period of "working through" and then a shift to a transference, say to a father or grandparent or other significant figure. Attachment research recognizes the nondominant strategy to be latent in an adult. Thus, in analysis a shift from one to another could be detected if, for example, the verbal pattern of preoccupied speech associated with one attachment figure is replaced by an avoidant dismissive pattern of discourse associated with another. Recognition of a shift is more difficult when the anxious-ambivalent strategy was established with both parents, as in the case of Mrs. S.

Desirable change is often signaled when a problematic form of communication like Mrs. S's pressured speech lessens or disappears. The lessening may result from implicit learning that such a self-protective aversive strategy is no longer needed in the supportive environment of the analysis. Implicit learning of this sort is greatly enhanced by explicit learning about what types of interchanges trigger the anxious excitement state.

I assumed that my silences or verbal interventions had a role in Mrs. S's episodic overexcitement and loss of focus. However, this common method of identifying analyst-induced sources of disruption failed appreciably to move us in the direction of positive change or of deeper understanding of the meaning of the disruptions. The communicative leap forward came about through the use of metaphors.

Mrs. S supplied the initial metaphor in her dream of using her basement for a child's playroom. In the immediate exchanges that followed my suggestion about touching or playing around her bottom, she responded with full collaborative sharing. Then, when Mrs. S returned to her excited state, I experienced an immediate frustration—"Oh, shit, here we go again"—with blame swinging back and forth between "I've lost her" (my failure) and "she's abandoning and thwarting me" (her antagonism). To this point the communication between us represented a coconstructed present, but what followed cannot be explained without recourse to our view of dreams, symbolism, metaphor, and the analyst's use of inner speech to explore an implicit message to himself.

We believe the four or five REM-state dreams experienced each night embody efforts to work over problems and dilemmas from the preceding day. When the dreams obtain consciousness through their imagery and especially the affects contained or associated, they provide internal communication to the dreamer. But with analysands, a dream dreamt, remembered, and related is also a component of the collaborative shaping of information within the analysis. When my attempt to shed light on the meaning of that information contained in the dream touched a responsive chord in Mrs. S, I was at first pleased and guardedly hopeful. However, in a short time, I was once again disappointed without a clue to explain the origin of the disruption. That is, I could not recognize an active triggering contribution on my part. I was left with the alternative—that my contribution to our dyadic pattern lay in my failure to apprehend the essence of the message contained in the message of pressured speech. I was therefore, intuitively searching for some as yet unrecognized basis in Mrs. S's lived experience that she was flagging for us. This search guided my inner monologue and created the basis for the crucial shift between "shit" as frustrated expletive to "shit" as metaphor for enema-induced explosive feces. I both created the metaphor and recognized its significance in Mrs. S's explicit message about her mother giving her enemas and her implicit message of looser and looser content. We believe that one of the great findings of psychoanalysis lies in the power of metaphor to form a link between verbal sequential speech and an imagistic use of language expressive of affect and body sensation.

An analyst's inner communication risks an idiosyncratic reading based on theory or personal proclivity. The excitement of discovery can easily lead to unwarranted conviction and the danger of suggestion.

I communicated my hypothesis in a straightforward manner with a slight questioning tilt in my voice at the end. What happened subsequently provides a way to evaluate the possibility of her making an inauthentic response. Initially she took up my suggestion with coherent associations and seemingly genuine interest. Then, unlike other times she did not become overexcited but rather returned to the topic in the next series of hours. Moreover, her responses to my interventions were contained and collaborative, adding to and amending my interpretations. Later, when I indicated that I assumed her dominant affect to her mother's enema initiative to have been anger at a bodily intrusion, she reacted with an immediate resort to pressured diffuse speech. When an intervention brought into awareness a crucial, lived experience, she could be genuinely collaborative, but when a false note was struck she evidenced no inclination to false intellectual compliance.

In the interchange, more was being expressed than an empathic failure leading to a disruption. The form of the disruption itself pointed to a role enactment involving welcome help and unwelcome intrusion. Our collaborative exploration of the enema experience had been analagous to her dominant experience of her mother's helping her to become regulated. However, my misreading of her affect as anger, reflecting my experience of her verbal barrages as intrusive and my personal resentment of bodily intrusions, was experienced by her enactively as an unwelcome dysregulating intrusion.

Middle Phase: Erotization

A transference struggle ensued concerning misrepresentations about her financial resources that she had made when arranging for a reduced fee. When I interpreted this enactment in terms of a retentive urge, her aggressive reaction to my "intrusion" emerged with a brief violent explosion of anti-Semitic feelings. The second transference struggle followed my calling to her attention an overpayment in her check. She complained that I was taking everything from her. I noted her disclaiming responsibility and suggested that she wanted my attention as she had her mother's. I interpreted her overpayment as an unconscious attempt to get me involved in checking on the quantity of her bowel movements. The next hour she described that she had begun to drink brandy when paying her bills. After a while she noticed that she felt both sick in her stomach and sexually aroused. She took a shower and was afraid someone like her mother would come in and find her sexually aroused. I suggested that in her verbal barrages she had exposed me to her state of uncontrolled excitement. If I took it as productive analytic work, I would in effect be reliving with her the myth she and her mother formed that enema overstimulation was healthful. Alternatively, if I did not collude with her in that way and recognized the experience as problematic for her, she could separate herself and join me in considering the meaning of the reenactment. She described how she wanted mother to know about her state of sexual excitement, but was afraid that if she did she would take it away. I acknowledged that what she remembered was that, rather than becoming angry, she had enjoyed the sensations and the intimacy during the enemas. Consequently her bowel and anal region, as well as the sensation of painful tension, had become sexualized and she had developed a sensual orientation toward her mother.

After this she reported an experience over the weekend with her husband. She had wanted to avoid intercourse but finally agreed. She had difficulty lubricating and was unresponsive until she began to fantasy that her husband was an aggressive woman who "knew her inside out." With that, she became tense, excited, and orgastic.

This whole period ended with a further secret being revealed. She had withheld all information about her concern with her daughter's bedwetting, tension, and separation anxiety. After an interpretation of the repetition of denied collusion between her mother and daughter, she arranged for her daughter to begin analysis.

Discussion 3

From early in life, essential features of communication are what to know and what to tell. Children determine whether their desires and the feelings they have about their parents are safe to acknowledge to themselves. And then they must assess how safe it is to let others know what they know about themselves and them. At each step in the process of knowing and telling, the possibility, even probability, of deception enters. For inner comfort, not to know that one is being deceptive, however otherwise maladaptive, is advantageous because the danger of shame or guilt at deceiving or withholding is averted. Messages encoded as bodily experience or body metaphors, enactive relational strategies, and nonverbal aspects of speech often shield the communicator (patient or analyst) from the recognition that a deception is being practiced.

Mrs. S's shift from explosive preoccupied speech to withholding and avoidance, while restricting the associative flow, opened the space for me to understand and comment on her need for privacy and secrecy. With this affirmation, the level of discourse moved upward, allowing her to be more reflective. She could venture to reveal to herself and to me the previously disavowed deception about her finances. Deception and revelation became dominant features of the subsequent communicative exchanges, and much of the process took place at an enactive level. A clash of self-interest about the fee itself required openness on both our parts about our desires. I wanted to be paid my full fee, and she wished to control her contents and tease me into pursuit. More broadly, when the context of analytic work is dominated by deception, one person becomes the detective ferreting out what the other is up to but won't "come clean" about. The other may regard himself as engaging in an innocent or righteously indignant cover-up. This inevitably interactional component requires the analyst to make a rapid shift between the position of sensing how the patient's self-interest seems to the patient from her perspective, and how it plays out as a way to compel the analyst into a role that neither is supposed to acknowledge.

The analyst faces risks no matter how he proceeds. The empathic perceptual stance risks collusion. The position of external observer risks finger-pointing trapping and condemning. The complexity of such impasses exceeds the either/or of perceptual positioning. If the patient's deception occludes inner knowledge, an empathic entry into her state of mind would be to this very lack of self-awareness. Consequently, "empathically" telling the patient what she doesn't let herself know becomes an authoritarian intrusion. So the technical principle governing timing is for the analyst to sense and infer from the verbal and nonverbal message as delivered whether knowledge previously unavailable to the inner world of metacognitive monitoring has come to assume a form that permits an analytic discourse about it. I believed that enough openness existed for Mrs. S to entertain the link from fee deception and overpayment to the attachment aspects of holding back and being teasingly inviting. Only when the message contained the reference to her sexual arousal in the shower did I believe inner awareness of the link to the eroticized nature of the attachment to her mother (not her father) was available to her. The issue before us was no longer self-unawareness but awareness that allowed for an interpretation of several levels of deception: the collusion with her mother to regard the enemas as health producing, the collusion about erotization of her relationship to her mother, and the blocked awareness of the significance of her and her own daughter's involvement in related symptomatic enactments.

Middle Phase: Dissociation

In the subsequent work Mrs. S's use of verbal barrages and disconnected contents had virtually disappeared. Now if she experienced my interpretations as holding her to some association or issue that was painful, she resorted to drowsiness and sleep. Her reaction of avoidance of "harsh reality" had been supported by both parents, father with global laxness and mother with her belief that every pain borne should be covered over by an oral treat. Each visit to the dentist was followed by a splurge at the confectioners. Her mother's version of this reaction to pain and stress was her drinking. Mrs. S associated her sleeping during the hours of analysis to her mother's alcoholic stupors. She explained that if I insisted that she take responsibility for something "too unpleasant to face without candy coating"; she would do to me what her mother did to her father when he made a demand on her. I believed this spontaneous association of Mrs. S to be accurate, but as I tried to use it, it seemed to provide little therapeutic leverage.

In the hour I am about to describe she began by saying that she was annoyed with herself for having fallen asleep during the previous session. She repeated her idea of being like her mother—ducking out of her responsibility by getting drunk. She reviewed again a memory, often evoked, of her mother looking lovely, all dressed for a party. Her father returned home from the office, late as usual. Instead of complimenting her mother as Mrs. S knew her mother craved, he admonished her to behave herself at the party and not drink too much. Mrs. S's heart sank because she knew what would happen. "Sure enough, by the time he came down her mother was gone, out of it—drunk again," and Mrs. S had to go with her father to the party while her mother slept it off.

Sensing Mrs. S's willingness to work toward an understanding of her sleeping, I was relaxed in my listening. Because the memory she associated to was familiar, I listened with particularly loose attentiveness. I pictured the scene described so often: the pretty, childishly sensitive mother waiting for her compliment; the ambitious, self-centered father, too worried about his career to notice or care, possibly preferring his daughter's adoring company anyway; the daughter consciously unhappy and unconsciously looking forward to her oedipal victory. As she said, "Sure enough, by the time he came down, mother was gone, out of it—drunk again," I had a series of associations: gone, out of it, absent, absences, hysterical absences, Charcot and Freud. "By the time he came down"—how much time? How much could the mother drink by the time he came down? How much effect could it have? My experience with Mrs. S was that it took her no time at all to be "gone, out of it—asleep again," if she perceived me to be like her thoughtless, demanding father. I emerged from this reverie with the construction that Mrs. S had consciously accepted her mother's myth of drunkenness, but had unconsciously perceived her to be employing a dissociative state. I conjectured that when she said she was identifying with her mother's drunken stupor, she was in fact identifying with her mother's dissociation perfumed with alcoholic vapors.

I suggested that when she connected her sleeping during the analytic hours to her mother's being drunk, she might be omitting a perception she had made and then blocked out of awareness. As she described the incident, it seemed to be as if she had perceived her mother as saying, "If I'm not told what I want to hear and need to hear in order to feel good, but am told what I don't want to hear about facing up, then I'll drop out of consciousness." I added that that seemed to correspond with the experience as she recreated it with me. She took up this suggestion actively and gave confirming evidence for my belief that her mother had only time for a drink or two while her father rapidly freshened up.

Mrs. S's sleepiness did not end with this understanding. The therapeutic effect lay in her changed attitude toward her drowsiness. Before she had treated sleepiness as comparable to a toxic alcoholic state—something that came over her, about which she could do nothing. Now she regarded being sleepy as something she did and as such something she could take responsibility for by cooperating actively in analyzing its multiply determined meanings.

Discussion 4

Observations based on the Strange Situation Test help to distinguish between avoidance as a strategy to preserve an insecure attachment and disorganization/dissociation as a consequence of failure to organize a coherent strategy. An avoidant child has learned not to risk an appeal for comfort or to venture an affective protest. The enactive communication of the avoidant pattern contains the deception to an observer that the child neither notices nor is troubled by the stress of the mother's departure. The falsity of this apparent dismissal lies in the fact that the child monitors the mother's departure and return in peripheral vision and responds with heightened autonomic nervous system responses and cortisol levels. For a presymbolic child, avoidant behavior constitutes a lived experience in the here and now, but the "plan" is not recognized as intentional or symbolized. Later a child or adult uses verbal symbol constructions such as "my mother was a saint and I'll discuss it no further." Or, a child will know that he is intentionally holding back his tears to not give an abuser the satisfaction of knowing he has hurt him.

Avoidance, dismissal, and disavowal restrict communication to others and to the self, but the strategy permits an uninterrupted lived experience and awareness of self. In contrast, dissociation interrupts a lived experience from which removal of the aware self seems the only solution. Through avoidance and restricted communication of need or protest, a child can stay clear of an angry caregiver or one who is in a constant overburdened state. A child, however, may be physically abused, frightened, severely shamed, or overwhelmingly overstimulated by the very person the child seeks for protection. Then the child becomes trapped between approaching or avoiding, leaving clicking off her being present as a last resource. In Mrs. S's childhood the father whom she would approach for protection and affection would sexually overstimulate her, and the mother who she would approach for safety and regulation would herself have "clicked off" and made the approach/avoid dilemma unresolvable.

For the purpose of communication, dissociation in the form of clicking off, whether into a trance, a substance induced "stoned," or suddenly asleep, constitutes a unique loss. The person—mother or patient—to be conversed with is physically present but cognitively and affectively absent. The colloquial expression is "nobody home." The first index on the frightening behavior scale is "parent suddenly completely 'freezes' with eyes unmoving, half-lidded." Among the AAI criteria for dissociation is falling silent in midsentence only to emerge later with loss of the original thought. The patient doesn't experience herself as having done anything, only as something having happened to her, often without warning and generally without choice or control. For Mrs. S, having her experience of clicking off into sleep linked with her mother's clicking off after her husband's shaming, helped her to recognize the many levels of communication in the model scene of going to the party. Mother was saying, "Don't look to me to be a protective maternal buffer between you and your seductive and dangerously abusive father; I dissociate and disappear." Father was saying, "See, we really do have a contract in which I can excite you or disappoint you at will." Both parents were saying, "We take no responsibility for what we do and you need not either." And in her falling asleep, Mrs. S was saying to me, "I will not let you spotlight issues that could shame, embarrass, humiliate, or frighten me. I will not let you try to hold me responsible. Like my parents I resolve dilemmas not by facing them but by 'checking out.'" By linking her sleep with her mother's "alcohol" dissociation, we lifted the message from a channel that had no possibility of recognizing an associational linkage to a triggering event. We moved to a message level in which the bodily channel could be recognized as a choice, resource, and strategy employed under particular circumstances that could be further analyzed.

Final Phase: Tenderness and Sensuality

In the terminal phase, three-and-a-half years after the analysis began, Mrs. S opened her Monday hour by describing a desire to withhold. She related a dream in which she entered Montaldo's Knick-Knack store. She was buying a vibrator for her mother. It was expensive, and she asked if anything was on sale. Yes, everything, the store was going out of business. On the shelf was a lovely china figurine she thought she would get for her daughter. There were also silly-looking owls. She hated them but thought she would buy them, although even in the dream she wondered why. She associated Montaldo/vibrator to a dildo and made some intellectual-sounding associations about the store going out of business being the analysis. I noted her lack of feeling and asked her about the urge she had said she had to withhold. She responded that she found it easier to talk about her dream intellectually than to tell me about a photograph she had taken that pleased her. It was a magnolia bud. She described in detail how she had arranged to get the lighting from the back so the petal opening could be seen. Inside was the soft, sticky bud itself, with a thin film of moisture that picked up the light.

In the background of my thoughts as I listened was my impression that photography was for her both a sublimation of voyeuristic tendencies and an attempt to resolve her conflicts about her self-worth. Having identified with her father's superficiality and exhibitionism, she had in dilettantish fashion dabbled at being a dancer, actress, pianist, and poet. Toward the end of the middle phase, she had taken up photography, which she believed to be an interest of mine. She attempted to approach photography with a depth approximating her idealized estimate of my expertise. She had been extremely reluctant to talk about her photographs, fearing competition or, worse, a superficially patronizing "That's nice." As she spoke, I visualized her narrowing her lens focus to the curve of a single bud. I conjectured that her resistance to talking about her creative effort had relaxed and that this indicated that she was gaining in her struggle to establish a more stable sense of self-worth. My attention was caught by the music in her voice—the unusual softness and gentleness—a soothing quality as she described the ever-so-slight stickiness and the light and shadows. A whole new image came into my mind: Mrs. S as a little girl ever so gently stroking her moist clitoris with a mixture of self-soothing and erotic pleasure. With this visualization a thought that had troubled me crystallized: while she was now heterosexually orgastic after years of total frigidity, her experience of heightened arousal, as she described it, had always seemed strained and tense, and her fantasies were never far from sado-masochistic trends.

During adolescence there had been a complete suppression of direct genital masturbation. In her first analysis, when as an adult she attempted genital masturbation for the first time, she had forcefully inserted a candle. We had come to understand that the repression of her childhood masturbation had occurred under the pressure of harsh reactions from her mother, reinforced by religious training and fixated by a displacement to her anus.

I concluded that despite the intermittent beneficial effect of this analytic work, she never consolidated a tender, gentle feeling toward her body.

I was jarred into awareness of the affective discrepancy between my image of the little girl tenderly stroking herself and Mrs. S's dominant state of mind when she made the slightly irritable comment that I would probably assume the bud was a penis. She spontaneously took up the issue of masturbation and mentioned that she is now conscious of the urge when she is alone. It is no longer shifted to her anal rubbing or to compulsive eating. But her fantasies during intercourse this weekend were of a cruel King and Queen who forced themselves on her. In her fantasy she resisted, and only then could she feel sexually aroused. I felt that my line of thought about gentle masturbation was out of keeping with her current emotion, and I asked her more about her fantasy. She said there was a painful build-up of tension and then an exciting release—as with the enemas. She associated to her dream, stating she could see how in the dream she arranged to increase her tension to enable herself to have the accompanying sexual sensation, but why would she want to buy the owl when she hated it. I said "Ow." She responded: "It hurts! Of course."

In the Tuesday hour, her associations to a dream about a see-through nighty went to her being excited, getting a man excited, followed by a strange feeling of drowsiness. I interpreted that she was building up a sequence in which she was excited, would get me excited, go to sleep, and—she filled in: I would attack her and she could do nothing about it. She recalled the excitement of baths with a boy cousin. It was her mother's message to her that she could look at her cousin until her eyeballs popped out, but don't touch. Go to sleep and if her cousin touched her that was OK, but don't touch herself and don't let it be known that her genital was excited.

In the Wednesday hour she began by talking about giving up in a game of tennis with her husband; he was so good and she was comparatively nothing. She added that I had helped her to know that she compared herself with her cousin and her father, and that when she admired their physiques she would fall into a hole of withdrawal. Even now it was hard to climb out. Reflecting to myself on her portrayal of me as having helped, I thought she would be receptive to an intervention reopening the issue of her body image and her self-depreciation. I reminded her of the photograph she had been reluctant to tell me about. Using words as close to hers as I could, I repeated what she had described. She said with some surprise that she had originally thought of the bud as a penis but as I redescribed it to her she had thought of it as a clitoris—especially the softness, And she added in a poignant tone that she didn't value what she had—she never thought of nice sensations she could get from her own body.

The next hour she related going to the theater and weeping through the last act during which the hero shows he is unable to accept aspects of himself. She thought of her father, and the feeling persisted. She can't stand herself for having these feelings. I suggested that she found it difficult to accept her soft, deep feeling toward her father. She agreed and, after a silence, thought of the photo of the bud (and the fuzzy soft substance). At the same time she felt a strong urge to wipe out these feelings. She said that it was easier to think of herself with a spotlight on her, becoming all excited. But when the light went off she felt flattened out. I suggested that since childhood her excitement had been for fantasized male qualities; that when she lost that feeling she felt flattened out as though she had no feminine body parts of value. She said that when she was growing up, she had liked playing with girls but when she came home she was afraid she'd be too soft for her father. She then described how yesterday she had been alone and felt tense and thought of masturbating. It was a mad kind of desire—angry and rough. I asked if the angry roughness might be to cover her desire to touch herself as if she were a little girl soothing herself very softly and gently. She nodded and fell silent and pensive. Then she said she didn't know why she was silent, as she didn't feel at all sleepy or resistant. I wondered if she might be giving herself a moment of privacy. She agreed, adding poignantly that she had never been really able to feel private, even with the door locked.

Discussion 5

In contrast to the gross impairment of communication created by dissociation, the communication illustrated in these hours can only occur in situations of secure mutual sharing and great familiarity. Mrs. S's rendering of her photograph had the quality for me of a musical aesthetic experience similar to listening to a symphony. In my reverie I entertained the mixture of beauty and eroticism present in a Mapplethorpe photograph of a calla lily. But with a very significant difference: the message contained in my reverie was not intended for my delectation, but rather subserved a shared spirit of inquiry that now guided our work. While my reverie state, and the imagery in it, was a communication to myself, it existed on a continuum of monologue-dialogue aimed at a shared revelation. Moreover, the communication to myself flowed from paralleling her imagery with mine in the interest of bringing into my awareness a troubling latent question: What made the sensual tenderness we were both experiencing different from any prior shared experience? The inherent motivation for analysis as an exploration gains focus from a compelling question that crystallizes in one or the other of the partners and then becomes shared. The question may be carried in the conscious inner monologue and accrues answers in imperceptible fragments of understanding. Or the question may become conscious more suddenly and dramatically—more like an Aha! experience in which an unformulated nagging doubt becomes a definable revelation.

As we talked about the dream and the photograph, I formulated to myself a question that gave substance to a doubt about Mrs. S's progress that previously I had been unable to conceptualize. Despite the progress she had made from frigidity to orgastic experience, did her path to sexual excitement still require the heightening of roughness and pain? A second question then followed: Was her capacity for sensual tenderness coming to the surface through the channel of the metaphor of a visual and auditory experience? Could she bridge the gap between a visual and auditory perception of a magnolia bud and a message in and to her body, especially in and to her genital? When and how might the metaphor and my understanding of it be presented to her to acti-vate the parallel body imagery in her inner monologue that I pre-sumed was, or might be, there?

Timing in love and war (and analysis) is everything, to amend an old cliché. When I was jarred out of the aesthetic and sensual pleasure of my reverie about the photograph and little girl's gen-tle genital self-soothing, I was instantly aware of Mrs. S's switch to her familiar provocative stance. A battle over "penis envy" as an explanation was a carry-over from her prior analysis during which a probably unempathic interpretation had provoked enact-ments rather than exploration and understanding. I noted she spontaneously related her dream to masturbation and joined her in exploring this theme that had a markedly different affective valence from my gentle sensual reverie. The return to her dream permitted me to offer her a different metaphor—the owl—ow—of hurt, of painful excitement. The next hour presented no bet-ter opportunity to link her description of the magnolia bud photograph with gentle genital stroking. In the third hour I believed she was communicating a readiness to consider the inter-pretation I had conceptualized based on her depiction of me as having been helpful to her in her struggle with envy. Her tem-pered idealization struck me as indicating that I could now test to see if the communicative channel between us was open. I chose to echo her description, using her own words but less musically, that is, more matter of factly, offering it to her as more a metaphor for her to reflect on than a formal interpretation. Her confirma-tion was startling and pleasing—a trigger for a remarkable sequence of working together closely. During this period of close sharing, the atmospheric quality (the analytic third) was fluid with chan-nels open to past and present. Ultimately the communication played out through a valuable paradox. We existed in closely shared back and forth understanding—a form of lively touching and reflecting and then in full sympathy opened ourselves up to a com-fortable separateness of selves, a togetherness in each retreating to a private domain of inner experience. In such a domain, com-munication of self to self predominates not only without loss of attachment but as an essential component of a secure attachment.

CHAPTER EIGHT

CONTROVERSIES AND ANSWERS: COMMUNICATION AND A SPIRIT OF INQUIRY RECONSIDERED

Insight and Relationship

The impetus for writing a book is generally to say no and yes. We want to say no to the polarization of insight and relationship. The debate has had its usefulness in bringing forth the previously unacknowledged power of relational elements during analytic therapy, so much so that it would seem in the view of many to be the central or dominant mode of bringing about change. Indeed, in many of our clinical examples we have described moments in which the relational connection—its disruption and repair—has been crucial in moving the treatment forward. In chapter 4 we have explicitly described a number of relational-centered moments (moments whose impact is conveyed through forms other than verbal meaning) as constituting the maximally effective aspect of the communication. Thus, we affirm the efficacy, the very necessity, of a cocreated relational experience that undergoes vicissitudes across a spectrum of motivational shifts. In chapter 5 especially, we explicitly defend the significance of verbal interchanges. In each chapter we illustrate the sorting out of meaning through associations, affects, dreams and the nuances of the way something is said or omitted.

Our aim is not to support either side of the argument but to suggest that the argument has run its course. We have tried to persuade the reader that it is more useful to recognize that in analytic therapy, communication comprises sharing information and sharing knowledge of the self to each other by talking and all other forms of relating. Both analyst and analysand gain insight about motives and intentions while creating the emotional, relational context favorable to insight and the emergence of new perspectives. Our yes is to the proposition that communication provides the overarching concept for what occurs in an analytic exploration. Relating is communicating the nature of the selves of patient and analyst in both their interplay and in the changes and revisions of self with others that constitutes the inner experience of each. Talking is communicating the nature of thoughts, images, and emotions in an active exchange that unconsciously shapes the receptivity of the listener. In the sense of the speaker's shaping effect on the listener, talking is relational. However, talking is telling the story the speaker has to tell to be known. The storyteller does so in a particularly precise manner that both informs the listener and connects (attaches) the listener to the speaker. Analytic practice has long emphasized the potentially defensive nature of speech, its capacity to hide and to deceive. Self psychology has rescued the message as delivered from the devaluation of overzealous defense interpretation. We have emphasized the nuance of spoken communication in the technical principle: "the message contains the message" that introduces chapter 7.

In chapters 1 and 2 we laid the groundwork for the development and significance of communication in early life. An argument for the importance of multifaceted forms of relating as compared to communicating by symbolic syntactical speech can draw on the richness of parent-infant interchanges. In all shared communication, emotional knowing evolves from vocal rhythm coordination, affective facial mirroring, and disruption and negotiating (Beebe and Lachmann, 2002). Indeed it can be argued that emotional knowing of another is always the music, not the words. We have argued that to formulate plans and intentions we need to know what to do with the emotional knowing we glean from the music. The use of structured language is then required to provide a frame, a context, and an orientation of time (past, present, and future). To be able to pause and reflect involves the self-regulation that permits inner speech to organize and reorganize motivational states, whether self is with other or self is alone in the presence of the other.

Mankind's unique creation is language, and language is a principal source of mankind's creativity. In analysis, moments of implicit relational learning and moments of explicit insight are creative highpoints of the talking to one another about what matters to and between analyst and patient. Although difficult to prove, we believe personal reflective space and analytic conceptual space is a product of the specific use of symbolic reasoning and the language needed to play conceptually with alternatives. A brief digression prompted by a television program on evolution that one of us (JDL) watched enables us to place our conceptualizations into an evolutionary perspective that links creativity, affectivity, and communication.

The success of Cro-Magnon man (our ancestors) over Neanderthals was attributed by the scholars to Cro-Magnon's development of symbolic communication. The earliest and latest burial sites of Neanderthals contained identical crude stone tools and no ornaments. The burial sites of Cro-Magnons contained tools evolving in complexity, jewelry, and daily items suggestive of a concept of an afterlife. Neanderthals were larger and more muscular and used spears they would push directly into their prey at close proximity and high risk. Cro-Magnon hunters used spears they could throw from a safer distance. Neither leave any record of writing or language but Cro-Magnon leaves the remarkably beautiful drawings of animals and occasionally people in caves in France and Spain. Platt (2001) writes, "For tough, outdoor type Cro-Magnons, creating the resulting animal portraits meant thinking about what animal to draw, how big or small, and what color to use. The process of drawing suggests these early artists had a concept of time (past, present, and future)." These characteristics are indicative of a heightened form of consciousness. "Cave art is the first hard evidence of mental image in the brain as we see it being transformed into a tangible image on a wall. The mental image supplies the models needed for creating artwork and eventually creating words" (p. 57). Platt distinguishes between communicating through sounds, grunts, and gestures and the evolution of language and speech. A long transition existed between artistic creativity in the form of cave drawings, burial ornamentation, and improved tools 40,000 years ago and the evolution of language at an unknown but relatively recent time. The amazing rate of cultural and technological change in the last 3000 years of known history has been associated not only with the human capacity for artistic creativity but with the meaning and signification provided by language and speech. Language gave to our ancestors and gives to us the ability to ask questions, formulate hypotheses, be precise with linear syntactic reasoning, and imaginative with symbolic play and metaphoric flights of fancy. Those are the attributions of communication that are furthered when analysis is conducted in a spirit of inquiry.

Commentaries based on evolution treat language and speech as tools of progress which indeed they are. However, in addition to technological and cultural progress we emphasize the role of language in the facilitation of collaboration and intimacy in family and groups. As we demonstrated in chapter 1, language is learned only in the intimacy of caregiver-infant relationships. We can speak of the circularity within communication of emotion-based relationships. The learning and usage of language opens each individual to enriched relationships with others and with himself or herself.

Provision and Inquiry

Another impetus for our book was a desire to consider the place of provision and inquiry during development and analysis. For over half a century the necessity for frustration or nongratification of "infantile" drive urges was accepted dogma for child-rearing and psychoanalysis. Believing that the pendulum had swung too far, analysts such as Winnicott (1953), Stone (1961), and Guntrip (1971) advised the maintainence of a physician-like attitude and a holding environment (see chapter 4, in the discussion of touch). In Kohut's early self psychology writings, a tension exists between his maintaining a construct of frustration and the dawning recognition of the significance of empathy: "the most important aspect of the earliest mother-infant relationship is the principle of optimal frustration" (1971, p. 64). Tolerable disappointments lead to building "internal structures which provide the ability for self-soothing and the acquisition of basic tension tolerance in the narcissistic realm" (p. 64). This drive theory holdover was overshadowed in this and Kohut's subsequent theory building by the significance given to empathy, defined as vicarious introspection. While defined by Kohut and subsequent writers (Lichtenberg, 1981; Schwaber, 1981) as a specific mode of perception or a listening stance, empathy in the view of many became something good a therapist said or did for a patient. To limit the definition of empathy to sensing into the state of mind of another rather than the use to which the information is put, Kohut used the extreme example of the Nazis being guided by knowing the emotional state of added terror the noise of Stuka bombers would produce. But the ambiguity remained between empathy defined as a specialized mode of gaining information about a patient's emotional-cognitive state and empathy loosely regarded as a panoply of analytic interventions that benefit the patient and move the treatment forward.

Frustration did not seem a good designator for either empathic perception or sensitive, vitalizing, or insight-producing interventions, and, appropriately, Bacal (1985) suggested optimal responsiveness as the listening perspective that better conveys Kohut's intention. The term responsiveness, however, has been used by those who advocate a "doing" stance rather than a listening perspective. Consequently, in analysis "the necessary" ambiguity between listening and doing is lost. Initially the listening side of the ambiguity contained in responsiveness received the most extensive study (Lichtenberg, Bornstein, and Silver, 1984). Gradually, self psychologists began to explore the "doing" aspects captured in such frequently used phrases as being empathic or making an empathic interpretation. Construing empathy as a therapeutic activity was a logical consequence of Kohut's portrayal of self pathology as the result of deficit. A portion of self-structure was missing, thus the deficit must be repaired. Kohut had two theories for the repair. One was that transmuting internalizations resulted from optimal frustration. The second was that empathic listening permitted archaic self-needs to come to the fore and be responded to by the mirroring, twinship, and idealizing experiences that were structural lacks. Initially, self psychologists in the tradition of ego psychology advised that the patient's need and desire for mirroring, twinship, and idealizing was to be interpreted, not provided. However, the idea of confining such responses to interpretations that produced "understanding" was an artificial and unworkable restriction. In actuality, analysts were providing patients with opportunities to experience the beneficial vitalizing or soothing effects of "being" mirrored, experiencing sameness, or feeling under the comforting protective umbrella of an idealized therapist. As analysts recognized that widely different needs, wishes, and desires came to the fore as the dominance of motivational systems shifted, the distinction between interpretation and either metaphoric or actual caregiving responses became further blurred. Lindon (1994) directly explored the place of provision, and Shane et al. (1997) proposed that successful analysis involved the provision of enhancing "new" relationships that the patient had never previously experienced.

A theory of deficit holds that for the patient to be able to progress developmentally, the analyst gives to the patient what the patient did not get. That is, the analyst "provides" in response to the need the patient indicates. This provision can be in the form of verbal responses or other new relational experiences. However, in a systems theory we construe the patient's indication of his needs as a metaphor for less than adequate forms of regulation that result not from deficit but from the manner in which he has organized prior experience. An anxious-resistant or an avoidantly attached infant could be regarded as having a deficit of experiences that would have led to a secure attachment.

However, from a motivational systems perspective, the infant and his caregiver have evolved a strategy that allows a form of relatedness based on self and interaction regulation that preserves their connection to each other at times of stress. Whatever the cost for infant and caregiver of richness and flexibility of intimacy, they maintain an attachment experience. Insecure attachment is not a deficit, it is a strategy to make the best of a less than ideal situation. Stated in adult terms, a preoccupied or dismissive state of mind with respect to attachment inclines a patient toward a particular mode of regulating his attachment needs and his manner of communicating. The patient's manner of regulating his attachment needs under stress both shapes the analytic interaction and provides patterns of verbal and nonverbal communication. These interactions are open to scrutiny on a moment-to-moment basis as illustrated by the interplay between Nick and his analyst in chapter 3.

Shifting from "deficit" to "regulation" does not eliminate the usefulness of provision as a way to conceptualize what caregivers and analysts do. The careful listening and use of humor (chapter 3), the use of touch and affective expression (chapter 4), the translation from body language to words (chapter 5), the metaphor of the kitten (chapter 6), and the recognition of the disturbed regulation of sensuality (chapter 7) indicate an inextricable mixture of inquiry and provision. However, we have redefined "need" and "provision" here. The needs conveyed and expressed by the patient are co-constructed by patient and analyst so that they "optimally" fall within the domain of analytic responsivity. Whatever the patient's needs, they are shaped in the analytic interaction to fit best the limits of "responsivity" of this analyst and this patient in this analysis. It would be ludicrous to say that Nick suffered from a deficit of humor and that the analyst had to make up for this deficit by providing Nick with humor. Rather, the developmental experiences that would simultaneously accrue to a secure attachment and a solid secure sense of self were absorbed into the analytic dyad. Humor was the metaphoric medium through which Nick's developmental patterns would be revisited, engaged, and reorganized. A different style by another analyst could have organized Nick's needs and their inclusion in the treatment process differently. Nonetheless we believe it is valuable to move from the immediate specific intersubjective context of infant-caregiver or analyst-patient to consider the more abstract guiding principle of a "spirit" of provision and a "spirit" of inquiry that augment each other.

We chose the term "spirit of inquiry" because it refers to a force both indefinable and influential. A "spirit of provision" offers a useful way to regard caregiving and the development of communication described in chapters 1 and 2. The attachment researchers George and Solomon (1999) state, "The child's attachment system is organized to *seek* protection from the attachment figure: in contrast the caregiving system is organized to *provide* protection for the child" (p. 625). We expand this statement: The child's motivational systems are organized to *seek*, that is, communicate the need for a wide variety of responses including protection; in contrast, the caregiving system is organized to *provide* recognition and responses to a panoply of innate and developing needs.

Broadly speaking, both Katie's and Kierra's mothers (chapters 1 and 2) were guided by a spirit of provision. Katie's mother's mode of provision was imbued by a highly sensitive attentiveness to Katie signalling that she was ready for another spoonful. Kierra's mother conscientiously provided a thorough bath and a patient feeding, but, exasperatingly to an observer, ignored the baby's ear-piercing cries and never noticed her own flaccid hand or Kierra's subsequent full eye and head aversion. A reciprocal inquiry about the other was strongly present between Katie and her mother and painfully absent between Kierra and her mother. We have different explanations for the disparity. Kierra's mother couldn't give her baby what she didn't have—a theory of deficit. Kierra's mother and Katie's mother were both operating on procedural memory, thus each automatically and unconsciously carried out complex actions and interactions based on their experience as recipient—a theory of unconscious regulation.

A third explanation reasons that the Katie-in-her-mother's-internal-experience-of-her was conceptualized (symbolized) as having an independent subjectivity so that an inquiry into that subjectivity flowed easily and naturally. In contrast the Kierra-in-her-mother's-internal-experience-of-her was conceptualized as an *object*, highly valued, and needing to be provided for to the best of her mother's ability. For Kierra's mother the spirit of provision lacked a spirit of inquiry into the state of mind of her baby that would be required for provision to be intersubjective rather than interactive. The symbolic encodings of self-with-daughter in the inner experience of the two mothers gave to the emotional exchange and physical holding a completely different feel. "The child's representation of himself and of his inner experience must be seen as a direct function of his *parents'* capacity to represent and imagine his mind and thus provide a secure base for him as a 'mentalizing' being" (Slade, 1999, p. 805).

Acceptance, Transparency, and Acceptability

The increased importance given to how significant others are held in mind and the influence such conceptions and preconceptions exert has led to more attention being paid to inner communication (metacognition) and to how knowledge of the other is obtained (mentalization). If we assume Katie's mother holds implicit or explicit conversations with Katie in her mind, we might imagine she may say "What a lovely little girl you are! I listen to you, you tell me what you like and need and don't like, and we have fun together." How does this Katie-held-in-mother's-head get transmitted to Katie? We see this as a process of acceptance, transparency, and acceptability.

Acceptance means "this baby of mine that I'm going to have or now have, she (he) is whom I want and love." Transparency means "I can let you know who you are to me, and who I hope and believe you will become. And I can let you know who I am and how I feel not only about you but about a lot of other people and things too." Acceptability means: "I know that what you observe and sense about me—me with you and me more generally—is not entirely under my control, but your acceptance of me and the you-in-my-mind comes about as an expression of your individuality. The extent to which you experience me as acceptable to you is a broad emotion extending over time while also subject to moment-to-moment fluctuations as your motivations and mine coincide and diverge."

For Katie's mother, the Katie-in-her-mind and the Katie-she-had were what she wanted to have and had. Her sense of Katie-for-her was conveyed through her glowing smiles and occasional frowns, the clear verbal and nonverbal cueing to Katie of what she wanted Katie to do, the anger at what she didn't want, and the coordination of her actions in response to signals from Katie. From what her mother made transparent, Katie could determine that her mother's self-interest was being affirmed by Katie and other aspects of her life, and her mother and she are what each wants the other and themselves to be.

For Kierra's mother, the Kierra-in-her-mind seemed to be more like an emotionless mechanical object to be scrubbed, fed, and played "at," not "with," while the Kierra-she-had emitted ear-piercing cries, vigorously turned head and eyes away, and played listlessly with a depressed look. Kierra could get no leads from her mother's expressionless face or indications of intentions that were in conjunction with hers. What Kierra could feel was the flaccid holding hand and the absence of expression, eye contact, and verbal communication. From this she might sense that her mother viewed her as an object without subjectivity; this she found unacceptable, and she turned away physically and off emotionally.

We can draw an analogy to the clinical situation where the therapist's holding of the patient-in-mind enters into the communication, shaping and being shaped by what each does with and to the other moment to moment. The analyst's acceptance is of both the patient who is and the person she can become. Freud and analysts since have more successfully expressed the essential humanity of patients-held-in-mind through case descriptions and accounts of dialogue (as with Nick in chapter 3) than they have in theories. Experience has demonstrated to us that, with some patients, we can easily observe our acceptance of the patient's essential humanity however expressed in aversiveness, self-centeredness, and demands. With other patients, the fluctuations in our acceptance may be signaled by boredom, revulsion, hatred, withdrawal, and wishes for the patient to leave. When the analyst can win the struggle with himself back to an essential acceptance—often by recognizing what aspect of his own humanity has become compromised—the treatment will take strides forward. The struggle with himself may be helped by consultation and dialogue but is dependent on the open inner communication of the therapist and his acceptance of his own humanity.

The significance of transparency has undergone a dramatic change, moving from a rigidly adhered to (at least in theory) anonymity to a broad discussion of disclosure (Renik, 1993). Transparency plays out in the analyst's acknowledged or disavowed revelation of who she is to the analysand and who the analysand is to her. We have recommended that analyst's "wear their patients' attributions" to discover how they have come across to the patients. A degree of transparency by both patient and analyst is necessary for analysis to take hold, and increasing the degree of transparency is a goal of the inquiry that constitutes the ongoing process. The ongoing process reveals not only the patient-in-mind of the analyst and the analyst-in-mind of the patient but small and large transformations of the view of each by the other and especially of the view of the two in interaction. Transparency depends on the openness and accessibility of each to inner communication about self-with-other and implicit or explicit communications to the other of the way in which he is being viewed. Experiencing the analyst as mean, unyielding, and dangerous may be signaled by the patient's dream image of a witch figure with bared teeth and communicated during the hour even before the dream is revealed by a rigid posture, clenched fist, shaky tone of voice, and eye avoidant entry. Alternatively, the analyst's anticipatory dread of his patient's sinking into depths of despair after a more revealing hour (chapter 6) would inevitably be exposed to her by the tensions of his body and speech, the low-keyedness of mood, and his greater hesitance—his "walking on eggs."

When brought into the open, the most opaque representations of self-with-other often have the greatest potential for effecting major change. Revelation often takes the path of long enactments involving rather fixed interactions as with Mrs. S's (chapter 7) obfuscating speech in the early phase and her falling asleep, checking out, and dissociation in the later phase. The puzzling over the experience, its repetition, the affects being triggered, its opacity, and the subtle cues could occupy either patient or analyst, preferably both, but wrestling with the ambiguities is primarily the responsibility of the analyst. We described the analyst's associations that gave him entry into his enacted "role" in the enema outpourings and his misreading of the "drunken" escape. Once recognized in his inner monologue, the work of explicit communication begins. The joint construction of model scenes provides a major link between what has been implicit and what can now be made verbally explicit.

The question of a patient's acceptability to an analyst is rarely discussed. As the patient reveals himself to the analyst at his "best" and at his "worst," can the analyst see herself responding to him without crippling aversiveness? Does the extent or particular form of the patient's antagonism, suicidal inclination, entitlement, blindness to the feelings of others, dishonesty, contempt, or obsequiousness get to the analyst to such a degree that she can view him in no other way than dangerous, evil, or despicable? Nick's analyst (chapter 3) and Sonya's analyst (chapter 6) had to work against being swept up in the outward manifestations of negative self-image in which each patient was enveloped.

We believe that acceptability in analysis requires the emergence and recognition of discrepant views of each by the other. Analysts must gain full awareness of both the troubled views of self held by the patient and another more actual or potentially esteem-building view. Sonya's analyst had to appreciate fully her hopelessness and desperation about relationships, especially with men, and yet see a Sonya in his mind's eye that could be loved and desired by a man. Indeed, the Sonya who could be loved had to be more than a "construct." The analyst had to feel the actuality without threat to his boundaries or hers. And, on the other side, Sonya had to view her analyst as unresponsive like her mother, ritualistically dutiful like her father, and helpless with her like both parents had been with her brother for Sonya to be able to experience at a given moment a discrepant, more positive, and effective view of the analyst. Such a moment of positive and effective communication occurred when the analyst brought together from sources unknown to him the bridging reflection, "You look like a sad little kitten." The communication of the negative or positive dominant view of the self and self-with-other by way of moods, body language, greetings and partings, glances and aversions, blushes and frowns, and little "meaningless" phrases dropped here and there is conveyed before, during, and after the words that define it explicitly.

Multiplicity of Self-Experience or Multiple Selves

The description we have given of discrepant views of self and the modes of their communication points to another controversy Kohut attempted to correct, namely, the experience-distant splitting up of the person into id, ego, and superego macrostructures. He pointed to the essential healthiness in nonpsychotic patients of a cohesive self existing in a sustaining self-selfobject matrix. Loss of cohesion with symptoms of fragmentation did occur, but with empathic resonance cohesion would be restored. We have argued in our writings on motivational systems that aspects of self and self-with-other differ considerably, depending on whether the dominant motivation is the need for physiological regulation, attachment, exploration, sensuality, sexuality or expression of aversiveness. At the same time we have supported Kohut's claim for the essential sameness in most instances of a sense of self (not a "structure" of self). Many clinicians, however, have emphasized the loss of cohesion in many pathological situations. The clinical findings of vertical splits in narcissistic patients (Kohut, 1971) and perversions (Goldberg, 1995), multiple discrepant working models of attachment (Bowlby, 1980), dramatic shifts of affect states in borderline patients, separated dissociative states, and multiple personality disorders attest to the frequency of loss of cohesion of the sense of self sometimes extending to the extreme of fractionation with "alters."

Mitchell (1993), in addition to other relational analysts (Bromberg, 1998), suggested that multiple selves are a more accurate portrayal of nonpathological states. However, we support the concept of a cohesive sense of self. We point to the maintenance of an experience of continuity of identity over time despite many changes (Lachmann, 1998). We also agree with Kohut's suggestions that integrative traits such as wisdom, humor, creativity, compassion, and spirituality are best conceptualized as indicative of a cohesive center of initiative. Alternatively, in our depiction of five complex motivational systems, we have contributed to the conception of a multiplicity of self-experience. This concept of multiplicity reflects two trends. First, a focus on moment-to-moment shifts in experience during analysis, an approach advocated by Kleinian, relational, and self psychologists, forces our recognition of how different the subjectivity of analysand and analyst can be as the intersubjective field alters self-experience. The second trend is the general recognition of the widespread existence of acute trauma arising from sexual and physical abuse, sudden danger, and unexpected loss, as well as from stress trauma arising from these disturbances during childhood and later that lead to insecure attachment and disorganized, disoriented, and dissociative states.

Communication differs in each of the conditions to which we have referred ranging from spare to effusive, collaborative to oppositional, dismissive to preoccupied. However when the sense of self is cohesive and integrative capacities are heightened, communication with the *self* is open, flexible, often rapid and spontaneous, even unexpected. This more intimate communication may involve words and images without the need of detailed syntax. However, to communicate to others the products of this inner creative awareness may require the full employment of language, metaphor, and other symbolic systems.

Conversational Space, Relational Space, and Conceptual Space

In moment-to-moment tracking of ordinary fluctuations of motivational dominance during analysis we observe changes in conversational space, relational space, and conceptual space. Conversational space refers to the opportunity a speaker provides for a listener to respond in a participatory collaborative manner. It begins with the pauses and turn taking of the earliest conversational runs between caregivers and infants described in chapters 1 and 2. Relational space refers to unique, cocreated patterns of being formed together by a dyad such as therapist and patient. Does one or the other control the relational space through intrusiveness, unavailability, domination, or submissiveness? The cocreated relational field may permit therapist and patient to observe himself, the other, and what they formed together—their joint creation. Or, patient, therapist or both may have his, her or their monitoring and reflective capacity compromised by strong affect states and rigidified enactments. In the latter case, conceptual space will be made opaque with patient, therapist, or both unable to allow playful fantasies, creative flights, and insights to flourish. The collapse of conceptual space is pathognomic of therapeutic impasses and the blocking effect of repeated dissociation, as with Mrs. S (chapter 7), in the middle phase.

With Sonya (chapter 6), conversational space initially would have been totally empty if the analyst had not done everything he could to fill enough of it to ever so gradually develop a relational space of safety and connection between them. Sonya appeared to block any use of conceptual space and while the analyst struggled to keep open his internal registry of their state together, the success of the struggle to form a utilizable conceptual space was evidenced by their coming together in the shared metaphor of the kitten. With Mrs. S (chapter 7) in the initial phase, she occluded the conversational space with her outpouring of words. The relational space was diverted by the "talk" being unconsciously directed to her prior analyst—a reflection of the unresolved loss of her father. In the end phase, the conversational and relational space had reached a level of sharing and knowing explicitly and implicitly how to be and work together. A rich conceptual space then opened to Mrs. S to relate her dildo dream and describe her magnolia photograph. Concurrently, the relaxed atmosphere facilitated the analyst's reverie about gentle masturbation. By tracking the closing and openings in their relaxed space, the analyst chose an opportunity in their conversational space to invite a joint conceptual expansion of insight.

The openness of conceptual space and the inner conversation that reveals its dynamics are essential to the discovery of who "resides" there and what multiple others can come into being. Sonya had a conviction of a Sonya who could not be helped and an analyst who could not and would not help along with a slowly emerging Sonya-kitten who could be "adopted" lovingly. Her analyst "knew" both Sonyas and added a Sonya who in his playful fantasy could someday be a loving and loveable romantic partner—in her words, her two "surprises" for him.

Conceptual space is of the greatest importance for transformative potentials to be released—the sensual and sexual gentleness of Mrs. S being a happy example. As Mrs. S described her photograph of the magnolia bud, the analyst's quiet unobtrusive listening opened access to her inner experience of body-self fantasy. At such moments, the analyst's focus shifts from interaction and active dialogue, allowing for a reverie state. During such an open free-formed conceptual space, either or both members of the dyad can gain access to memory, loosely formulated streams of thought, and emerging fantasy. The analyst's fantasy of the little girl's gentle stroking of her clitoris illustrates the closely engaged with and yet disengaged from the other that can occur in this type of open conceptual space and quiet nonintrusive listening.

Trauma and Talk

In contrast to the rich potential of a stable secure relational space, trauma closes off conceptual space and exerts a paradoxical effect on the role of talk in "talk therapy." Trauma destroys the sense of safety in an event associated with the trauma and at a minimum compromises basic trust (Erikson, 1959). Relational space is thus filled with the central issue of the restoration of trust and security of attachment. The traumatized patient consequently peeks outward from a protective self-centered focus with little room for appreciation of the subjectivity of the therapist. Conversation is compromised by preoccupied or dismissive patterns of speech, or, when too close to the traumatic area, lapses in orientation to time, place, or person. Talk is then more like an enactment of the problem than a source of narrative information in itself. In addition, if in consequence of a perceived empathic failure, the experience of the trauma is being reenacted relationally, affects may mount to states that obliterate conceptual space or affective experience may be so blocked that a deadened detachment or dissociation renders empty of meaning the cognition that takes place.

Nonetheless, we believe that verbal communication is essential to the resolution of the effects of trauma. In his discussion of a presentation of the case of Harry (chapter 5), Jaenicke (2001) took up our question, "Why talk at all?" Jaenicke writes:

> One characteristic of traumatized patients and especially those prone to "somatization, detachment, and dissociation like Harry" is that linkage is experienced as dangerous. Whether it be linkage between the psyche and the soma, between the conscious and the unconscious, between affect and thought, between one form of defensiveness and another, between ties and self-integrity, between themselves and others, or between themselves and the analyst, words serve the important double function of identifying self-states and bridging the gaps. Verbal linear exchanges have the functions of: "placing in context, highlighting and fixing in memory, opening to alternatives, and scaffolding for reflectedness in inner speech" [pp. 314–315; quoted material in this passage is from chapter 5, this volume].

Jaenicke adds that he regards the main function of words to be a medium of empathy. He refers to our statement in chapter 5: "When a patient feels [that] his motives, as they come to make sense to him, are thoroughly understood and appreciated by the therapist, he can spontaneously enlarge his perspective to consider alternatives previously discarded or never entertained." In our view, words are not the only means of communication by which the analyst's empathic understanding is conveyed, but the verbal exchanges do provide a more precise defineable vehicle than facial expression, body gestures, ums and ahs, and simple echoing phrases.

And with empathy we return to a discussion of inquiry and provision. Empathy underlines the inseparability of the two. Systematically sensing into the state of mind of a patient is a powerful means of inquiring about the problems, past experiences, and strengths the patient has—as well as who the analyst is to the patient and who the patient believes he is to the analyst. At the same time, the results of the analyst's empathic inquiry are a powerful means of providing the patient with sustaining vitalizing or soothing. For a patient, sensing that her intentions and beliefs are being appreciated with increasing accuracy is essential to containment of disruptions and affect storms. Nonetheless, some activities of an analyst are more in line with caregiver provisions. The analyst's explanation to Harry of the nature of the flu and his use of his body symptoms to express distress was provision, not inquiry. So does provision come and go? Yes, at moments analyst and patient may be seeking opportunities for what the patient will experience directly as provision. But at most moments, we believe that the analyst (and at times the patient) seeks opportunities for what the patient will experience as an exploration conducted in her behalf, a provision for her essential well-being.

Finally, analysts, like caregivers, must be primed by their prior experience to form relationships, encourage communication, and provide what is needed to promote safety and stability. But ultimately for the difficult work of analysis, the sustaining capacity resides in the analyst's overriding spirit of inquiry. This sustaining spirit allows us to persist through the unknown, the confusing, the false sense of too easy knowing, and the torturous channels of disruptions that seem to occur without an apparent source. Through empathy and sustained inquiry, we gain tiny footholds in the uniqueness and complexity of individual and dyadic experience.

REFERENCES

Amsterdam, B. & Levitt, M. (1980). Consciousness of self and painful self-consciousness. *The Psychoanalytic Study of the Child*, 35:67–84. New Haven: Yale University Press.

Aron, L. (1999). *A Meeting of Minds.* Hillsdale, NJ: The Analytic Press.

Atwood, G. (2001). Shattered worlds/Psychotic states. Paper presented at the meeting of the Eastern Division of the International Council for Psychoanalytic Self Psychology, Toronto, February 3.

——— & Stolorow, R. (1984). *Structures in Subjectivity.* Hillsdale, NJ: The Analytic Press.

Bacal, H. (1985). Optimal responsiveness and the therapeutic process. In: *Progress in Self Psychology. Vol. 1,* ed. A. Goldberg. Hillsdale, NJ: The Analytic Press, pp. 202–227.

——— (1997). Optimal responsiveness and analytic listening: Discussion of James L. Fosshage's "Listening/experiencing perspectives and the quest for a facilitating responsiveness." In: *Conversations in Self Psychology: Progress in Self Psychology, Vol. 13,* ed. A. Goldberg. Hillsdale, NJ: The Analytic Press, pp. 57–68.

——— ed. (1998). *How Therapists Heal Their Patients.* Northvale, NJ: Aronson.

Balint, M. (1952). *Primary Love and Psycho-Analytic Technique.* London: Tavistock.

——— (1968). *The Basic Fault.* London: Tavistock.

Beebe, B., Jaffe, F. & Lachmann, F. (1992). A dyadic systems view of communication. In: *Relational Perspectives in Psychoanalysis*, ed. N. Skolnick & S. Warshaw. Hillsdale, NJ: The Analytic Press, pp. 61–81.

Beebe, B. & Lachmann, F. (1994). Representation and internalization in infancy: Three principles of salience. *Psychoanal. Psychol.*, 11:127–166.

——— & ——— (2002). *Infant Research and Adult Treatment: Co-constructing Interactions*. Hillsdale, NJ: The Analytic Press.

——— ——— & Jaffe, J. (1997). Mother–infant interaction structures and pre-symbolic self and object representations. *Psychoanal. Dial.*, 7:133–182.

Benjamin, J. (1988). *The Bonds of Love*. New York: Pantheon Press.

——— (1990). An outline of intersubjectivity: The development of recognition. *Psychoanal. Psychol.*, 7:33–46.

——— (1995). *Like Subjects, Love Objects*. New Haven, CT: Yale University Press.

Bion, W. (1962). *Learning from Experience*. London: Heinermann.

Bloom, L. (2000). Pushing the limits on theories of word learning. *Monogr. Soc. Res. Child Devel.*, 65:124–135.

Bowlby, J. (1958). The nature of a child's tie to his mother. *Internat. J. Psycho-Anal.*, 39:350–373.

——— (1969). *Attachment and Loss, Vol. 1*. London: Hogarth Press.

——— (1973). *Attachment and Loss, Vol. 2*. New York: Basic Books.

——— (1980). *Attachment and Loss, Vol. 3*. New York: Basic Books.

Breckenridge, K. (2000). Physical touch in psychoanalysis: A closet phenomenon? *Psychoanal. Inq.*, 20:12–20.

Breuer, J. & Freud, S. (1893–1895). Studies on hysteria. *Standard Edition*, 2:1–309 London: Hogarth Press, 1955.

Bromberg, P. (1998). *Standing in the Spaces*. Hillsdale, NJ: The Analytic Press.

Brooks, J. & Lewis, M. (1976). Visual self recognition in infancy: Contingency and the self-other distinction. Presented at Southeastern Conference on Human Development, Nashville, TN, April.

Bruner, J. (1983). *Child's Talk*. New York: Norton.

Bucci, W. (1997). *Psychoanalysis and Cognitive Science*. New York: Guilford.

——— (1997). Patterns of discourse in "good" and troubled hours: A multiple code interpretation. *J. Amer. Psychoanal. Assn.*, 45:155–188.

Clyman, R. (1991). The procedural organization of emotions: A contribution of cognitive science to the psychoanalytic theory of therapeutic action. *J. Amer. Psychoanal. Assn.*, 39(Supplement):349–382.

Cohen, J. & Squire, L. (1980). Preserved learning and retention of pattern-analyzing skill in amnesia: Dissociation of knowing how and knowing that. *Science*, 210:207–209.

Damasio, H. (1999). *The Feeling of What Happens*. New York: Harcourt Brace Jovanovich.

Damon, W. (1988). *The Moral Child*. New York: Free Press.

Davies, J. (1994). Love in the afternoon. *Psychoanal. Dial.* 4:153–170.

Davis, J. (2001). Revising psychoanalytic interpretations of the past: An examination of declarative and non-declarative memory processes. *Internat. J. Psychoanal.*, 82:449–462.

Edelman, G. (1987). *Neural Darwinism*. New York: Harper & Row.

——— (1992). *Bright Air, Brilliant Fire*. New York: Basic Books.

Ehrenberg, D. (1992), *The Intimate Edge*. New York: Norton.

Emde, R. (1988). Development terminable and interminable: 2. Recent psychoanalytic theory and therapeutic considerations. *Internat. J. Psycho-Anal.*, 69:283–296.

Erikson, E. (1959). Identity and the life cycle. *Psychol. Issues, Monogr. 1*. New York: International Universities Press.

Ferenczi, S. (1933). Confusion of tongues between adults and the child. In: *Final Contributions to the Theory and Technique of Psychoanalysis*, ed. S. Ferenczi. London: Hogarth Press, pp. 156–157.

——— (1953). *The Theory and Technique of Psychoanalysis*. New York: Basic Books.

Fishman, G. (1999). Knowing another from a dynamic systems point of view: The need for a multimodal concept of empathy. *Psychoanal. Quart.*, 68:376–400.

Fivaz-Depeursinge, E. & Corboz-Warnevy, A. (1999). *The Primary Triangle*. New York: Basic Behavioral Science.

Fogel, A. (1993). Two principles of communication: Co-regulation and framing. In: *New Perspectives in Early Communicative Development*, ed. J. Nadel & L. Camaioni. London: Routledge.

Fonagy, P. (1993). The roles of mental representations and mental proceses in therapeutic action. *The Psychoanalytic Study of the Child*, 48:9–48. New Haven: Yale University Press.

——— (1999). Memory and therapeutic action. *Internat. J. Psychoanal.*, 80:215–223.

Fosshage, J. (1994). Toward reconceptualizing transference: Theoretical and clinical considerations. *Internat. J. Psycho-Anal.*, 75:265–280.

——— (1995a), Countertransference as the analyst's experience of the analysand: Influence of listening perspectives. *Psychoanal. Psychol.*, 12:375–391.

———— (1995b). Interaction in psychoanalysis: A broadening horizon. *Psychoanal. Dial.*, 5:459–478.

———— (1997). Listening/experiencing perspectives and the quest for a facilitative responsiveness. *Conversations in Self Psychology: Progress in Self Psychology, Vol. 13*, ed. A. Goldberg. Hillsdale, NJ: The Analytic Press, pp. 33–55.

———— (1999). Forms of relatedness and analytic intimacy. Presented at the Annual Conference of the Psychology of the Self, Toronto, October.

———— (2000). The meanings of touch in psychoanalysis: A time for reassessment. *Psychoanal. Inq.*, 20:21–43.

Frank, K. (1999). *Psychoanalytic Participation*. Hillsdale, NJ: The Analytic Press.

Friedman, L. (1978). Trends in psychoanalytic theory of treatment. *Psychoanal. Quart.*, 47:524–567.

Freud, S. (1900). The interpretation of dreams. *Standard Edition*, 4 & 5. London: Hogarth Press, 1953.

———— (1916–1917). Introductory lectures on psycho-analysis, Part 3: General theory of the neuroses. *Standard Edition*, 16:243–463. London: Hogarth Press, 1963.

Gabbard, G. (1994). Commentaries on papers by Tansey, Davies, and Hirsch. *Psychoanal. Dial.*, 4:203–213.

Gelb, P. (1982). The experience of nonerotic contact in traditional psychotherapy: A critical investigation of the taboo against touch. *Dissert. Abstr.*, 43 248B.

Gedo, S. (1979). *Beyond Interpretation*. New York: International Universities Press.

George, C. & Solomon, J. (1999). The development of caregiving: A comparison of attachment theory and psychoanalytic approaches to mothering. *Psychoanal. Inq.*, 19:618–646.

Glover, E. (1955). *The Technique of Psycho-Analysis*. London: Bailliere, Tindall & Cox.

Goldberg, A. (1995). *The Problem of Perversion*. New Haven: Yale University Press.

Greenberg, J. & Mitchell, S. (1983). *Object Relations in Psychoanalytic Theory*. Cambridge, MA : Harvard University Press.

Guntrip, J. (1971). *Psychoanalytic Theory, Therapy, and the Self*. New York: Basic Books.

Gutheil, T. & Gabbard, G. (1993). The concept of boundaries in clinical practice: Theoretical and risk-management dimensions. *Amer. J. Psychiat.*, 150:188–196.

Hamilton, V. (1996). *The Analyst's Preconscious*. Hillsdale, NJ: The Analytic Press.

Hartmann, F. (1999) Dreams contextualize emotion: A new way of understanding dreams and dream symbolism. *Psychoanal. Dial.*, 9:779–788.

Hebb, D. (1949). *The Organization of Behavior*. New York: Wiley.

Hesse, E. & Main, M. (2000). Disorganized infant, child and adult attachment. *J. Amer. Psychoanal. Assn.*, 48:1097–1178.

Hoffman, I. (1983). The patient as interpreter of the analyst's experience. *Contemp. Psychoanal.*, 19:389–422.

Holder, A. (2000). To touch or not to touch: That is the question. *Psychoanal. Inq.*, 20:44–64.

Hollich, G., Hirsh-Pasek, K. & Golinkoff, R. (2000). Breaking the language barrier: An emergent coalition model for the origins of word learning. *Monogr. Soc. Res. Child Devel.*, 65:1–123.

Horton, J., Clance, P., Sterk-Elifson, C. & Emshoff, J. (1995). Touch in psychotherapy: A survey of patients' experiences. *Psychotherapy*, 32:433–457.

Jacobs, L. (1998). Optimal responsiveness and subject-subject relating. In: *How Therapists Heal Their Patients*. Northvale, NJ: Aronson.

Jaenicke, C. (2001). Discussion of Joseph D. Lichtenberg's *Transference as Communication: The Language of the Body*. *Selbstpsychologie*, 5/6:311–315.

Jaffe, J., Beebe, B., Feldstein, S., Crown, C. & Jasnew, M. (1999) Rhythms of dialogue in infancy: Coordinated timing and social development. *Monogr. Soc. Res. Child Develop.*, 66(2) Serial No. 264, pp. 1–132.

Kaye, K. (1982). *The Mental and Social Life of Babies*. Chicago: University of Chicago Press.

Knoblauch, S. (1996). The play and interplay of passionate experience: multiple organizations of desire. *Gender Psychoanal.*, 1:323–344.

——— (2000). *The Musical Edge of Therapeutic Dialogue*. Hillsdale, NJ: The Analytic Press.

Kohut, H. (1959). Introspection, empathy, and psychoanalysis. *J. Amer. Psychoanal. Assn.*, 7:459–483.

——— (1971). *The Analysis of the Self*. New York: International Universities Press.

——— (1977). *The Restoration of the Self*. New York: International Universities Press.

——— (1981). Lecture presented at the Annual Conference on Self Psychology, Berkeley, CA, October.

———— (1982). Introspection, empathy and the semicircle of mental health. *Internat. J. Psycho-Anal.*, 63:395–408.

———— (1984). *How Does Analysis Cure?* ed. A. Goldberg & P. Stepansky. Chicago: University of Chicago Press.

Lachmann, F. (1998). From narcissism to self psychology to . . . ? *Psychoanal. & Psychother.*, 15:5–27.

———— (2001). *Transforming Aggression.* Northvale, NJ: Aronson.

———— & Beebe, B. (1992). Reformulation of early development and transference: Implications for psychic structure formation. In: *Interface of Psychology and Psychoanalysis*, ed. J. Barron, M. Eagle & D. Wolitzky. Washington, DC: The American Psychological Association, pp. 133–153.

Lachmann, F. & Lichtenberg, J. (1992). Model scenes: Implications for psychoanalytic treatment. *J. Amer. Psychoanal. Assn.*, 40:117–137.

Lazar, S. (1998). Optimal responsiveness and enactments. In: *Optimal Responsiveness*, ed. H. Bacal. Northvale, NJ: Aronson.

LeDoux, J. (1996). *The Emotional Brain.* New York: Touchstone.

Levenkron, H. (in press). The analyst's affective honesty in the therapeutic action of psychoanalysis.

Levenson, E. (1983). *The Ambiguity of Change.* New York: Basic Books.

Levin, F. (1991). *Mapping the Mind.* Hillsdale, NJ: The Analytic Press.

Lewis, M. & Brooks-Gunn, J. (1979). *Social Cognition and the Acquisition of Self.* New York: Plenum Press.

Lichtenberg, J. (1981). The empathic mode of perception. In: *Self and Motivational Systems.* Hillsdale, NJ: The Analytic Press.

———— (1989). *Psychoanalysis and Motivation.* Hillsdale, NJ: The Analytic Press.

———— (1994). How libido theory shaped technique (1911–1915). *J. Amer. Psychoanal. Assn.*, 42:727–740.

———— (1999). Listening, understanding and interpreting: Reflections on complexity. *Internat. J. Psychoanal.*, 80:719–737.

———— & Meares, R. (1996). The role of play in things human. *Psychoanal. & Psychother.* 13:3–16.

———— Bornstein, M. & Silver, D., eds. (1984). *Empathy I & II.* Hillsdale, NJ: The Analytic Press.

———— Lachmann, F. & Fosshage, J. (1992). *Self and Motivational Systems.* Hillsdale, NJ: The Analytic Press.

———— ———— & ———— (1996), *The Clinical Exchange.* Hillsdale, NJ: The Analytic Press.

Lindon, J. (1994). Gratification and provision in psychoanalysis. Should we get rid of "the rule of abstinence"? *Psychoanal. Dial.*, 4:549–582.

Little, M. (1966). Transference and borderline states. *Internat. J. Psycho-Anal.*, 47.

—— (1990). *Psychotic Anxieties and Containment.* Northvale, NJ: Aronson.

Loewald, H. (1960). On the therapeutic action of psychoanalysis. *Internat. J. Psycho-Anal.*, 41:6–33.

Lyons-Ruth, K. (1999). The two-person unconscious: Intersubjective dialogue, enactive relational representation, and the emergence of new forms of relational organization. *Psychoanal. Inq.*, 19:576–617.

Mahler, M. (1968). *On Human Symbiosis and the Vicissitudes of Individuation.* New York: International Universities Press.

McLaughlin, J. (1995). Touching limits in the analytic dyad. *Psychoanal. Quart.*, 64:544–565.

—— (2000). The problem and place of physical contact in analytic work: Some reflections on handholding in the analytic situation. *Psychoanal. Inq.*, 20:65–81.

Main, M. (2000). The organized categories of infant child and adult attachment. *J. Amer. Psychoanal. Assn.*, 48:1055–1096.

Meares, R. (1993). *The Metaphor of Play.* Northvale, NJ: Aronson.

—— (2000). *Intimacy and Alienation.* London: Routledge.

Miller, J. (1985). How Kohut actually worked. In: *Progress in Self Psychology, Vol. 1,* ed. A. Goldberg. New York: Guilford, pp. 13–32.

Mintz, E. (1969a). On the rationale of touch in psychotherapy. *Psychother.: Theory, Res. & Practice,* 6:232–234.

—— (1969b). Touch and the psychoanalytic tradition. *Psychoanal. Rev.*, 56:365–376.

Mitchell, S. (1988). *Relational Concepts in Psychoanalysis.* Cambridge, MA: Harvard University Press.

—— (1993). *Hope and Dread in Psychoanalysis.* New York: Basic Books.

Modarressi, T. (1980). An experimental study of "double" (amphiscious) imagery during infancy and childhood. Presented at meeting of American Psychoanalytic Association, New York, December.

—— (1981). An experimental study of mirror imagery during infancy and childhood: The evolution of the self and its developmental vicissitudes (unpublished).

—— & Kenny, T. (1977). Children's response to their true and distorted mirror images. *Child Psychiat. Human Develop.*, 8:94–101.

Modell, A. (1994). Memory and the psychoanalytic cure. *Canad. J. Psychoanal.*, 2:89–102.

Nelson, K. (1986). *Event Knowledge: Structure and Function in Development.* Hillsdale, NJ: Lawrence Erlbaum Associates.

Orange, D. (1995). *Emotional Understanding*. New York: Guilford Press.

Papousek, H. & Papousek, M. (1975). Cognitive aspects of preverbal social interaction between human infant and adults. In: *Parent-Infant Interaction* (Ciba Foundation Symposium). New York: Associated Scientific Publishers.

Pedder, J. (1986). Attachment and new beginning: Some links between the work of Michael Balint and John Bowlby. In: *The British School of Psychoanalysis*, ed. G. Kohon.

Pizer, B. (2000). Negotiating analytic holding: Discussion of Patrick Casement's *Learning from the Patient. Psychoanal. Inq.*, 20:82–107.

Platt, P. (2001). Cave art and the origin of speeches. *J. Cosmos Club*, Washington, DC, 11:55–58.

Renik, O. (1993). Analytic interaction: Conceptualizing technique in the light of the analyst's irreducible subjectivity. *Psychoanal. Quart.*, 62:553–571.

——— (1998). Getting real in analysis. *Psychoanal. Quart.*, 67:566–593.

Ruderman, E. (2000). Intimate communications: The values and boundaries of touch in the psychoanalytic setting. *Psychoanal. Inq.*, 20:108–123.

——— Shane, E. & Shane, M., eds. (2000), On Touch in the Psychoanalytic Situation. *Psychoanal. Inq.*, 20:1–186.

Sander, L. (1983). To begin with—Reflections on ontogeny. In: *Reflections on Self Psychology*, ed. J. Lichtenberg & S. Kaplan. Hillsdale, NJ: The Analytic Press, pp. 85–104.

——— (1997). Paradox and resolution. In: *Handbook of Child and Adolescent Psychiatry*, ed. J. Osofsky. New York: John Wiley, pp. 153–160.

Sandler, J. & Rosenblatt, B. (1962). The concept of the representational world. *The Psychoanalytic Study of the Child*, 17:128–145. New Haven, CT: Yale University Press.

Savage-Rumbaugh, E., Murphy, J., Sevcik, R., Brakke, K., Williams, S. & Rumbaugh, D. (1993). Language comprehension in ape and child. *Monogr. Soc. Research Child Development*, 58, 3/4.

Schacter, D. & Tulving, E. (1994). What are the memory systems of 1994? In: *Memory Systems*, ed. D. Schacter & E. Tulving. Cambridge, MA: MIT Press, pp. 1–37.

Schlesinger, H. & Appelbaum, A. (2000). When words are not enough. *Psychoanal. Inq.*, 20:124–143.

Schore, A. (1994). *Affect Regulation and the Origin of the Self*. Hillsdale, NJ: Lawrence Erlbaum Associates.

Schwaber, E. (1981). Empathy: A mode of analytic listening. *Psychoanal. Inq.*, 1:357–392.

——— (1998). Interview with Dr. T. Jacobs in the Newsletter of the American Psychoanalytic Association. *Amer. Psychoanalyst*, 32:23–27.

Shane, M., Shane, E. & Gales, M. (1997). *Intimate Attachment: Toward a New Self Psychology*. New York: Guilford Press.

——— ——— & ——— (2000), Psychoanalysis unbound: A contextual consideration of boundaries from a developmental systems self psychology perspective. *Psychoanal. Inq.*, 20:144–159.

Siegel, D. (1999). *The Developing Mind: Toward a Neurobiology of Interpersonal Experience*. New York: Guilford Press.

Siegel, E. (1984). *Dance Movement Therapy: Mirror of Our Selves*. New York: Human Sciences Press.

Slade, A. (1999). Representation, symbolization, and affect regulation in the concomitant treatment of a mother and child: Attachment theory and child psychotherapy. *Psychoanal. Inq.*, 19:797–830.

Slavin, M. & Kriegman, D. (1998). Why the analyst needs to change: Toward a theory of conflict, negotiation, and mutual influence in the therapeutic process. *Psychoanal. Dial.*, 8:247–284.

Slochower, J. (1996). *Holding and Psychoanalysis*. Hillsdale, NJ: The Analytic Press.

Spitz, R. A. (1957). *No and Yes*. New York: International Universities Press.

——— (1965). *The First Year of Life*. New York: International Universities Press.

Squire, L. (1994). Declarative and nondeclarative memory: Multiple brain systems supporting learning and memory. In: *Memory Systems*, ed. D. Schacter & E. Tulving. Cambridge, MA: MIT Press, pp. 203–232.

Stark M. (1999). *Modes of Therapeutic Action*. Northvale, NJ: Aronson.

Stern, D. (1997). *Unformulated Experience*. Hillsdale, NJ: The Analytic Press.

Stern, D. N. (1983). The early development of schemas of self, of other, and of various experiences of "self with other." In: *Reflections on Self Psychology*, ed. J. Lichtenberg & S. Kaplan. Hillsdale, NJ: The Analytic Press.

——— (1985). *The Interpersonal World of the Infant*. New York: Basic Books.

——— (1990). *Diary of a Baby*. New York: Basic Books.

——— Sander, L., Nahum, J., Harrison, A., Lyons-Ruth, K., Morgan, A., Bruschweiler-Stern, N. & Tronick, E. (1998). Noninterpretive mechanisms in psychoanalytic therapy: The "something more" than interpretation. *Internat. J. Psycho-Anal.*, 79:903–922.

Stern, S. (1994). Needed relationships and repeated relationships. *Psychoanal. Dial.*, 4:317–345.

Stolorow, R. & Atwood, G. (1992). *Contexts of Being: The Intersubjective Foundation of Psychological Life.* Hillsdale, NJ: The Analytic Press.

———— & Lachmann, F. (1984/1985). Transference: The future of an illusion. *The Annual of Psychoanalysis,* 12/13:19–37. Hillsdale, NJ: The Analytic Press.

———— Brandchaft, B. & Atwood, G. (1987). *Psychoanalytic Treatment, An Intersubjective Approach.* Hillsdale, NJ: The Analytic Press.

Stone, J. (1961). *The Psychoanalytic Situation.* New York: International Universities Press.

Sullivan, H. S. (1962). *Schizophrenia as a Human Process.* New York: Guilford.

Suttie, I. (1935). *The Origins of Love and Hate.* London: Kegan Paul, Trench, Trubner.

Thelen, E. & Smith, L. (1994). *A Dynamic Systems Approach to the Development of Cognition and Action.* Cambridge, MA: MIT Press.

Teicholz, J. (1999). *Kohut, Leowald, and the Postmoderns.* Hillsdale, NJ: The Analytic Press.

Tolpin, M. (2001). Enhancing the therapeutic experience from the self psychology forward edge perspective. Paper presented at the 24th Annual International Conference on the Psychology of the Self, San Francisco, November 10.

Tomkins, S. (1962). *Affect, Imagery, Consciousness, Vol. 1.* New York: Springer.

———— (1963). *Affect, Imagery, Consciousness, Vol. 2.* New York: Springer.

Tronick, E., Bruschweiler-Stern, N., Harrison, A., Lyons-Ruth, K., Nahum, J., Sander, L. & Stern, D. (1998). Dyadically expanded states of consciousness and the process of therapeutic change. *Infant Mental Health J.,* 290–299.

Vygotsky, L. (1962). *Thought and Language.* Cambridge, MA: MIT Press.

Wachtel, P. (1980). Transference, schema and assimilation: The relevance of Piaget to the psychoanalytic theory of transference. *The Annual of Psychoanalysis,* 8:59–76. New York: International Universities Press.

———— (1993). *Therapeutic Communication.* New York: Guilford.

Weiss, J. & Sampson, H. (1986). *The Psychoanalytic Process.* New York: Guilford.

Westen, D. (1999), Scientific status of unconscious processes: Is Freud really dead? *J. Amer. Psychoanal. Assn.,* 47:1061–1106.

Winnicott, D. (1953). Transitional objects and transitional phenomena. In: *Collected Papers.* London: Tavistock, 1958, pp. 300–305.

——— (1958). *Collected Papers.* London: Tavistock.

——— (1960). Ego distortion in terms of the true and false self: In: *The Maturational Processes and the Facilitating Environment.* New York: International Universities Press, 1965, pp. 140–152.

——— (1965). *The Maturational Processes and the Facilitating Environment.* New York: International Universities Press.

Zahn-Waxler, C. & Radke-Yarrow, M. (1982). The development of altruism: Alternative research strategies. In: *The Development of Prosocial Behavior*, ed. N. Eisenberg. New York: Academic Press, pp. 109–138.

INDEX

abstinence, 55–56, 71, 72, 98
acceptance, transparency, and
    acceptability, 180–184
Adult Attachment Interview (AAI),
    10, 31–32, 41, 150–151,
    157, 165
affect intensity, 28
affect regulation, 94
affective experience, multiple
    coding of, 109–110
affective states, intense, 127
agency, 31. *See also* intention
ambivalent-anxiously attached
    children, 47. *See also*
    anxious-resistant
    attachment
Amsterdam, B., 39
analyst-patient touch. *See* touch
analyst(s). *See also specific topics*
  affective participation, 88–93
  as "model"/"teacher," 75
  participation in analytic
    interaction, 56
  self-communication, 9
  sense of efficacy, 131
  silence and abstinence, 55, 56,
    71–72, 98
anonymity, 89–91, 182. *See also*
    self-disclosure
anxious hypervigilant observers, 34

anxious-resistant attachment, 33,
    151. *See also* ambivalent-
    anxiously attached children
Appelbaum, A., 98
Aron, L., 89, 90, 95
attachment, 95
  anxious-resistant, 33, 151
  avoidant, 33–34, 47, 164
  at one year, and its intersubjective
    communication, 31–35
  secure, 30
  and triadic communication, 27
attachment experience,
    analyst's trying to foster a
    minimal. *See* Sonya
attachment needs, regulating,
    178
attachment theory, 12, 94,
    177–179
attunement, 24–25, 118
Atwood, G. E., 57, 75, 76, 79, 84,
    89, 94
authenticity of analyst, 89
autobiographic self, 48–53
"autonomous" parents, 32
aversive motivational system, 151
avoidance, 123–126, 143, 145,
    164–165
avoidant attachment, 33–34, 47,
    164

transmuting internalization,
177
transparency, 180–184
trauma. *See also* sexual abuse
and sense of self, 51–52
and talk (therapy), 187–189
trauma survivors, and analyst-
patient touch, 101–102
triangular family system, 25–27
Tronick, E., 57, 69, 77–80, 83,
90, 116, 117, 121
"true" self, 24. *See also* false self
Tulving, E., 78
twinship transference, 63, 72

unformulated experience, 116

Vygotsky, L., 40, 44

Wachtel, P. L., 78, 90
Weiss, J., 47, 62, 78
Westen, D., 77
Williams, S., 41
Winnicott, D. W., 24, 75, 98, 110,
176
words, 142
as designators, 122–126,
143–145

Zahn-Waxler, C., 33